THE LIFE OF
CAPTAIN CIPRIANI

| | | | |

THE C. L. R. JAMES ARCHIVES
recovers and reproduces for a contemporary
audience the work of one of the great intellectual figures of the twentieth-century, in all
their rich texture, and will present, over
and above historical works, new and current
scholarly explorations of James's oeuvre.

Robert A. Hill, Series Editor

THE LIFE OF
CAPTAIN CIPRIANI

An Account of British Government in the West Indies

| | | | |

WITH THE PAMPHLET

The Case for West-Indian Self Government

C. L. R. JAMES

With a New Introduction by Bridget Brereton

DUKE UNIVERSITY PRESS   DURHAM AND LONDON   2014

© 2014 Duke University Press
All rights reserved

Designed by Amy Ruth Buchanan
Typeset in Arno Pro by Westchester Books Group

Library of Congress Cataloging-in-Publication Data
James, C. L. R. (Cyril Lionel Robert), 1901–1989.
The life of Captain Cipriani : an account of British govern-
ment in the West Indies, with the pamphlet The case for
West-Indian self government / C.L.R. James ; introduction
by Bridget Brereton.
pages   cm — (The C.L.R. James Archives)
Includes bibliographical references and index.
ISBN 978-0-8223-5639-4 (cloth : alk. paper)
ISBN 978-0-8223-5651-6 (pbk. : alk. paper)
1. Cipriani, Arthur Andrew, 1875– . 2. Trinidad and
Tobago—Politics and government. 3. West Indies,
British—Politics and government. 4. Great Britain.
Army. British West Indies Regiment. I. James, C. L. R.
(Cyril Lionel Robert), 1901–1989. Case for West-Indian self
government.   II. Title.   III. Title: Case for West-Indian
self government.   IV. Series: C. L. R. James Archives (Series)
F2121.J36 2014
972.9'04—dc23
2014017562

Cover photo courtesy of the *Trinidad and Tobago Guardian.*

CONTENTS

The Texts

C. L. R. James wrote *The Life of Captain Cipriani: An Account of British Government in the West Indies* almost certainly between 1929 and 1931 in Trinidad. When he left for England in February 1932, the manuscript had been completed—one of three manuscripts he took with him, the others being his only novel, *Minty Alley*, and much of what would subsequently become *Cricket and I* by Learie Constantine, a book largely written by James.

In Nelson, Lancashire, where Constantine and his family had lived for a few years, the book was privately printed by a small local firm, Coulton & Co., in the middle of 1932. Constantine provided the funds, and James and some new friends in Nelson made up parcels of the printed book to send off to Trinidad and other places in the West Indies and to radical booksellers in London and other British cities. The book comprised 107 pages and was dedicated to Constantine. It sold for one shilling and six pence in Trinidad.

Its circulation in Britain was presumably quite limited, but Leonard Woolf, co-owner with his famous wife, Virginia, of the progressive Hogarth Press, heard about it. He asked James to abridge the book drastically, cutting out nearly all of the biographical sections related to Cipriani and concentrating on the general attack on crown colony government. The abridgement was done in Nelson, James wrote decades later, and he "travelled up and down from Nelson to London to make all the arrangements for the publication." The result was a thirty-two-page pamphlet, entitled *The Case for West-Indian Self Government*, issued by the Hogarth Press, London, in 1933. It was number 16 in the series Day to Day Pamphlets—previous pamphlets had been authored by such luminaries as John Maynard Keynes and Harold Laski—and sold for one shilling (James 1932, 1933, [1963] 1993: 119–21; Constantine 1933; Worcester 1996: 22–24; Dhondy 2001: 40–41).[1]

James begins *Life* by stating that he was writing a political biography of the Trinidadian labor and political leader always known as Captain Cipriani, not as an account of his personal life but "as the best means of bringing before all who may be interested the political situation in the West Indies today" (James 1932: 1). The book marked his first effort to analyze history and politics through biography, a methodology that (as will be discussed later) was to be used frequently in his later writings. The dialectical relationship between leader and social or political movement—whether it was Toussaint, Lenin, Trotsky, or Nkrumah—was to engage his interest for the rest of his life.

The first chapter of *Life* analyzes the state of society in contemporary Trinidad (Tobago is not mentioned). Each sector—the colonial Englishmen; the white Creoles; the "coloured people," by which James means those of African and part-African descent—is subjected to acerbic sociological scrutiny. This chapter contains a justly famous, much quoted description of shade prejudice and social snobbery among the people of mixed African-European descent. Just one brief paragraph deals with the Indo-Trinidadians, composing at least one third of the island population by 1930; James believed that there was "no communal problem," no antagonism between "Negroes" and "Indians" in the West Indies. As several commentators have pointed out, here, as later in *Case*, James sweeps under the carpet the issue of ethnic divisions, specifically African-Indian divisions, which would dominate politics in Trinidad (and Guyana) in the period after World War II (James 1932: 1–19; Ledgister 2010: 92).

Chapters 2 and 3 provide information about Cipriani's life up to the outbreak of World War I in 1914, when he was already nearly forty, and about his activities during the war. It was as an officer in the British West Indies Regiment that he first came to public notice, when he courageously defended the men under his command, all volunteers, from the outrageously racist treatment they received at the hands of the military authorities.[2] This experience politicized the Captain, a white man from an elite Creole family of Corsican descent, and launched him on his career as the leader of the Trinidad Workingmen's Association (TWA), the most important labor organization in the colony during the 1920s and early 1930s. The TWA is the focus of chapter 4. (James wrongly asserts that Cipriani became president of the TWA in 1919; in fact it was not until 1923 that the TWA leadership offered, and Cipriani accepted, the presidency; James 1932: 20–49).

The longest chapter, and in many ways the heart of *Life*, deals with Cipriani's efforts to achieve legislative reforms to benefit the masses as an elected member of the colonial Legislative Council from 1925 (chapter 5). This section includes a brilliant analysis of the motivations and psychology of the nominated "unofficial" members of the Council and their hostility to the wider public interest as upheld, usually alone, by the Captain. Up against the governor and the British officials, these nominated members, and often his fellow electives too, it was almost impossible for Cipriani to achieve substantive legislative reforms in the interest of the working people. In the legislature he was "an influence more than a force," James concludes, meaning that while the Captain changed the tone and content of political discourse, both inside and outside the Council, he was rarely able to secure tangible changes (James 1932: 50–70). Cipriani also operated in the City Council of the capital, Port of Spain, which he used as another forum to confront the colonial government and work for the people. Chapter 6 details a famous struggle over the city's electricity franchise which he waged against the government and the business interests it favored (71–81).

Another struggle was over the government's attempt to introduce modern divorce legislation, detailed in chapter 7. This fairly long chapter was to attract a great deal of criticism from James's contemporaries when the book was published. A bill to allow divorce under the same conditions as in Britain at the time was first introduced in the Council in 1926, and Cipriani, following the official TWA position, supported it. In the face of intense opposition from the powerful Catholic clergy, the government withdrew the bill but reintroduced it in 1931. At this point, under huge pressure from the Church and from his fellow French Creoles, Cipriani defied the TWA line—still in favor of the Divorce Bill or at least neutral—and instead passionately supported the Catholic opposition. This alienated many key TWA leaders, especially its Indo-Trinidadian vice president, Sarran Teelucksingh, whom the Captain actually assaulted physically over the issue. Teelucksingh left the TWA, and so did several hundred Indian members, a huge blow to TWA's efforts to create a multiethnic base. Cipriani's actions in 1931 also alienated the local intelligentsia, who saw divorce legislation as progressive and "modern," and the non-Catholic TWA leaders. His stand seriously weakened the TWA and damaged his own prestige. The contortions that James goes through in this chapter, seeking to justify Cipriani's actions, were ridiculed by several reviewers of the book in 1932 (James 1932: 82–100; Neptune 2007: 21–26; Singh 1994: 150).

Finally, the last chapter (8) provides a brief personal sketch of Cipriani as a man and a leader; it includes a long extract from a speech he made at the British Labour Party's Commonwealth Conference in 1930. This, perhaps, is the only section of *Life* where James can be fairly accused of uncritical adulation or hagiography. Interestingly he concludes the book with a promise to produce a "second volume" on crown colony government in the West Indies, its historical evolution, the differences between the colonies, and the only "solution"—a volume that never in fact appeared (James 1932: 101–7).

The much shorter abridgement published in 1933 duplicates material from *Life* but excludes nearly all the material on Cipriani himself. The first section of *Case* reproduces much of the earlier analysis of Trinidadian and West Indian society found in the first chapter of *Life*. The second and third sections deal with the working of crown colony government in Trinidad, condensing material in pages 50 to 81 of *Life* (James 1933: 1–30). The only new material in *Case* is to be found in the last pages, where James makes an explicit, and impassioned, plea for London to acknowledge the "fitness" of West Indians for self-government and to grant it forthwith (30–32).[3]

It must be understood that both *Life* and *Case* are essentially political, in fact polemical, works. The purpose of *Case* was self-evident, as signaled by its title: to argue for the grant of self-government ("Dominion status") to the British West Indies. But the larger work should also be seen as an intervention in a political campaign. James used Cipriani and his struggles against the colonial establishment as the "hook" with which to make the case that the people of Trinidad and Tobago, and by extension all British West Indians, were ready for Dominion status and were being misgoverned under the existing system of crown colony rule. It is not an objective or even a deeply researched or scholarly biography of Cipriani—whose political career, in any case, was only at its halfway point in 1932. (He remained active in public life until his death in 1945.) And as I will argue later in this essay, it is essentially an "apprentice" work, lacking the profound original research behind *The Black Jacobins* or the mature insights and brilliant writing style of *Beyond a Boundary*. Yet *Life* and *Case*, polemical works written by James at the start of his long literary and political career, remain of great interest to students of the Caribbean nationalist movement in the first half of the twentieth century and, of course, to students of James himself.

James, Cipriani, and Trinidad, 1919–1932

C. L. R. James was born in 1901 into a highly "respectable," lower-middle-class black Trinidadian family of Barbadian origins.[4] His father was a teacher and a headmaster; both his grandfathers were skilled artisans who had emigrated from Barbados in the late nineteenth century. His mother was a housewife, a stylishly dressed woman who read widely and constantly, unlike his father. This was a religious (Anglican), status-conscious, and somewhat snobbish family. After attending primary schools his father headed or in which he taught, James won a coveted "exhibition" (free place) to Queen's Royal College, Trinidad's only government secondary school, a prestigious English-type grammar school for boys. He was a pupil here from 1911 to 1918; he has famously written about the school and its impact on him in *Beyond a Boundary* (and elsewhere; Worcester 1996: 3–10; James [1963] 1993: 29–30).

During the period between his leaving school (1918) and his departure for England (1932), James earned his living by teaching—at different times at a private high school; at his alma mater, Queen's Royal College; and at the Government Teacher Training College—and private tutoring. But the twin passions of his life at this time were literature and sports. He read very widely and consciously prepared himself to become a writer, of both fiction (short stories and a novel) and nonfiction (journalism and *Life*). He has described this period of his life in his classic *Beyond a Boundary* and in other writings (James [1963] 1993: 64–65, 111–16).

By the time he left Trinidad early in 1932, James had published at least five short stories, both locally and in British and American collections, and had also completed his only novel, *Minty Alley*, often described as the first full-length "barrack-yard" fiction from the British West Indies. No subsequent novel appeared, and James was to abandon fiction for political and historical writing after he left Trinidad. But the stories and the novel were an important part of his development as a professional writer (Worcester 1996: 18–21; Ramchand 1971: 5–15; Fraser 2008).

As a young man in Trinidad, James had made himself into a writer, trying his hand at several different genres: short fiction, a novel, political and polemical essays, book reviews, sports journalism, a full-length biography (Cipriani's), and a "ghosted" autobiography (Constantine's). I should make it clear, however, that this introductory essay to his *Life of Cipriani* does not engage with his writing and rhetorical techniques as displayed in that work. That would be an interesting and probably rewarding project, but my concern here is different: to understand why James chose to write a biography of Cipriani, to examine how it was received in Trinidad, and to assess its significance both for early West Indian nationalist thought and for James's own development as a historian, a Marxist theorist, and a cultural commentator.

James was born and raised in a British Caribbean colony that had developed a considerable intellectual and literary tradition by the early twentieth century.[5] Trinidadians of European, African, and "mixed" descent, living mainly in the colonial capital, Port of Spain, were writing on the history, culture, geography, and natural resources of their island. (Indo-Trinidadians entered this project later.) The capital had a public library, first established in 1851 and housed in a handsome neoclassical building opened in 1901, and a museum; a lively newspaper press had existed and flourished, despite Trinidad's status as a crown colony, since the mid-nineteenth century.

The island's most important intellectual and writer in the later 1800s was certainly John Jacob Thomas, about whom James was to write an admiring essay in 1969. Thomas was a largely self-educated scholar, teacher, and author, born around 1840 probably to former slaves. He was a leading member of Port of Spain's small group of literati and a frequent contributor to the island newspapers in the 1870s and 1880s. But he is best known for his two books. *The Theory and Practice of Creole Grammar* was a pioneering study of the Créole or Patois spoken by most Trinidadians when it was published locally in 1869. Thomas wanted to celebrate the language spoken by his compatriots, to dispel the notion that it was "*only* mispronounced French," fit only for illiterate peasants. But he was also interested in Patois as a linguistic phenomenon a century before Creole studies became fashionable in the academic world (Thomas [1869] 1969b).

When J. A. Froude's famously racist (and politically reactionary) diatribe about the British West Indies appeared in 1887, Thomas determined to answer it. His *Froudacity: West Indian Fables Explained* was published in 1889, just weeks before his death. It is a remarkably wide-ranging attack on Froude's account of people and politics in the colonies, especially Trinidad. In part it falls into the genre of "Vindication of the Race" works: Thomas defends the progress of black West Indians since Emancipation, despite the oppression and discrimination they faced everywhere. In part it is a sophisticated attack on crown colony government in Trinidad and on the "rubbish" London had sent out as governors, administrators, and legal officers. It is especially striking for its early expression of Pan-African views: James was to write, "He is as confident as Marcus Garvey, and is far stronger in history" (Thomas [1889] 1969a; James 1969; see also Smith 2002; Brereton 1977; Cudjoe 2003: 184–92, 298–306).

Though Thomas stands out in Trinidad's developing literary and intellectual tradition of the late nineteenth century, he was not alone. The island's newspaper press around this period was lively, remarkably uninhibited, and often interested in debates about culture, race, education, colonialism, and the like. Thomas himself contributed frequently to the papers owned or edited by black or mixed-race men and edited a short-lived literary magazine in 1883. Many articles, op-ed pieces, letters to the editor, and literary reviews engaged with often controversial issues, such as race prejudice and discrimination against black Trinidadians and the arrogance and incompetence of British colonial officials (an important theme in *Froudacity*). Though legislation like the Seditious Publications Ordinance (1920) attempted to curb the antigovernment press after World War I, in the years of James's youth the island possessed two daily papers, as well as smaller weekly journals such as the *Labour Leader*, to which he contributed (Brereton 1979: 94–109; Cudjoe 2003: 218–26, 271–74).

By the turn of the century several educated black Trinidadians had come under the influence of early Pan-African thinking. Henry Sylvester Williams, who organized the first Pan-African Conference in London in 1900, was a Trinidadian lawyer, and his visit to his native island in 1901 resulted in the formation of several branches of his Pan-African Association there. Though he spent most of his adult life abroad, and the Association soon faded in Trinidad, he was much admired by his race-conscious compatriots. Williams was almost certainly the model for Rupert Gray, the hero of the novel of that title published locally in 1907 by the Trinidadian Stephen Cobham. This novel clearly fits into the category of "Vindication of the Race" and reflects the spirited efforts—in fiction and in nonfictional polemical literature—of Trinidadians to defend "their people" from the pervasive ideological and institutional racism of the day (Cobham [1907] 2006; Mathurin 1976; Cudjoe 2003: 362–72; Rosenberg 2007: 25–32; Smith 2013: 71–83). In his own way James would also engage in this project in the post–World War I period.

But perhaps what was most important to his trajectory as a young writer was his close involvement with a small group of equally young intellectuals and aspiring writers, which has come to be known as the *Beacon* group after the literary magazine of that name, which they produced in the early 1930s. The leading members of the group were white or near-white, notably the Trinidadians of Portuguese ancestry Albert Gomes and Alfred Mendes; James was one of the few black participants. He was an important contributor to its activities. They met often, talked endlessly, exchanged books and records, and critiqued each other's writings. As James wrote decades later, perhaps tongue in cheek, "We lived according to the tenets of Matthew Arnold, spreading sweetness and light and the best that has been thought and said in the world" (James [1963] 1993: 64).

Even before the *Beacon* first appeared in 1931, James and Mendes collaborated to produce two issues of a small, cheaply produced magazine, *Trinidad* (December 1929 and April 1930). It featured poems, stories, and essays. Some of the stories were about Trinidad's working poor, including James's well-known "Triumph," a piece that has been seen as "programmatic" for the genre later known as "barrack-yard fiction," to which his novel *Minty Alley* also belongs. Gomes, who like Mendes was better off financially than James, launched the *Beacon* in 1931; Mendes was his chief collaborator. Since the 1970s scholars have consistently identified these two "little magazines" as marking a new epoch in Trinidadian and Anglo-Caribbean literature (Sander 1978, 1988; Rosenberg 2007: 123–58).

Thus there can be little doubt that writing his stories and novel, set in the urban barracks of Port of Spain, helped to stimulate James's political consciousness and his interest in the "poor and the powerless" of his island.

Of the group of young men who formed the *Beacon* coterie, Mendes seems to have been closest to James. Recalling James at this time, Mendes writes in his autobiography drafted in the 1970s, "He stood about six feet three inches, as lean as a pole, and possessed the kind of rough charm that women of all complexions succumb to so easily. His intelligence was of the highest order, his memory for music and literature phenomenal; all of this seasoned with a sharp wit and a sardonic sense of humour. . . . His life was free and untroubled, his obsessions, books and cricket. . . . I date my meeting him as the early beginning of the intellectual group he and I brought together and nurtured to a maturity that pioneered a West Indian literature" (Mendes 2002: 72). With his relatively secure financial situation, Mendes built up a large library and record collection, and the group often met at his house (or sometimes in James's room), free to borrow and listen to his books and records. Mendes and James were writing their novels (*Pitch Lake* and *Minty Alley*) at the same time, and they "fell into the habit of reading chapters to each other as the two books developed from week to week." The two aspiring authors no doubt influenced each other's development as writers; both novels—*Pitch Lake* was published two years before *Minty Alley*, both in England—can be seen as barrack-yard fiction, though Mendes's was more overtly preoccupied with race, which, according to him, was why James "did not like my novel" (Mendes 2002: 81–82).

The company of Mendes, Gomes, and the other young men making up the *Beacon* group must have stimulated James's development as a writer, a reader, and an all-round intellectual and cultured person. He was a nongraduate teacher and tutor, whose salary could only have been small, so the opportunity to borrow books, magazines, and records from his better-off friends must also have been important to him. Moreover some members of the group, notably Gomes, held fashionable left-wing views and claimed to admire the USSR and its experiment with communism. Regular discussions on world affairs and the ideological clashes of the period must have helped to stimulate James's political thinking, though his commitment to Marxism would develop only after he had left Trinidad. In any case he became widely known among the intelligentsia of Port of Spain as a learned and cultured man, exceptionally well-read, and a versatile writer.

James was also practicing his craft as a journalist during this period. He frequently wrote articles on sports, especially cricket, for the colony's newspapers and also unsigned pieces for the *Labour Leader*, the TWA's weekly paper, from 1922 to early 1932. He was a regular contributor to the *Beacon* in 1931–32. In 1931 one of his *Beacon* pieces earned him considerable fame: he replied at some length to an offensively racist article by Sydney Harland, a scientist at the Imperial College of Tropical Agriculture, which purported to establish scientifically the innate mental inferiority of the "Negro." According to James himself, the piece made him the talk of the town and even engaged the nervous attention of the governor and his executive council (Harland 1931: 25–29; James 1931a: 6–10; James [1963] 1993: 113–14).

Sports was his other passion in these years, football but above all cricket, which he played regularly at club level. A famous section in *Beyond a Boundary* describes the array of sporting clubs in the Port of Spain of the 1920s, each catering to men of a slightly different class or color segment, and his own choice—after much agonizing—for Maple, the club of the brown middle class, over Shannon of the black lower middle class. Significantly he quotes at length in this section his earlier account in *Life* of black-brown relations in Trinidad circa 1930, presumably to help his British readers understand the situation (James [1963] 1993: 51–53).

James always insisted that he had virtually no interest in local politics until soon before his departure for England (James 1962: 17; James [1963] 1993: 65). Though the "race question" was obviously an issue for him, as the Harland exchange makes clear, James has written that neither the race nor the "national" (colonial) question played a major role in his life at this time. Of course, his education had been thoroughly British, he was in awe of British literature, and most of his close friends were white or near-white. In an often quoted passage from his refutation of Harland, James wrote in 1931, "I am not 'touchous' on the race question. If at times I feel some bitterness at the disabilities and disadvantages to which my being a negro has subjected me it is soon washed away by remembering that the few things in my life of which I am proud, I owe, apart from my family, chiefly to white men . . . who have shown me kindness, appreciation, and in more than one case, spontaneous and genuine friendship" (James 1931a: 10; James [1963] 1993: 29–30; see also Worcester 1993: 54–80).

But many later commentators have doubted that James was as indifferent to local politics in this period as he has claimed. He must have been very much aware, for instance, of the serious urban unrest in 1919–20, mostly played out in Port of Spain, where he lived, and he later wrote that he knew a few of the leaders through cricket.[6] Indeed he wrote that it was cricket that brought him to politics; "injustice in the sphere of sport," especially discrimination against talented black cricketers, fired up his indignation: "Cricket had plunged me into politics long before I was aware of it. When I did turn to politics I did not have too much to learn"—a very Jamesian assertion. One biographer thinks that by the early 1920s, "he began to nurture a pronounced dissatisfaction with the restrictions placed on an educated black man in colonial society"; the roots of his anticolonialism lay "in his formative personal experiences on the playing fields and as a reader." After all, he read Garvey's *Negro World* as well as high-brow British periodicals, and he listened to calypso as well as the classics. Another biographer speculates that his barrack-yard stories and novel helped to fuel at least a literary radicalism and that he may have discovered Thomas's *Froudacity* in the 1920s, also contributing to a political awakening; as I have noted, he wrote an admiring introduction to the 1969 reprint of that classic work, first published in 1889 (James [1963] 1993: 65; Worcester 1996: 11, 14; Dhondy 2001: 26; James 1969: 23–49).

Certainly by the late 1920s, if not before, James and his circle were fascinated by the Captain, the white "French Creole" who had unexpectedly emerged as the leader of the TWA and the colony's pro-labor, anticolonial movement. James in particular "greatly admired this white man who introduced trade unionism to Trinidad's workers," according to Alfred Mendes. James himself told Paul Buhle a couple of years before his death that Cipriani never encouraged him to take part in politics—he was a "literary" man, and as a public servant, teaching at Queen's Royal College and the Training College, he was not allowed to be publicly involved in political movements. He wrote in *Beyond a Boundary* that he was never a "follower" of Cipriani, nor officially a TWA member. But he said in the 1987 interview with Buhle, referring to himself in the third person, "James was part of the movement. . . . Cipriani would come to me and ask me what about this and so on. . . . I would speak on behalf of the movement." Clearly the two accounts are somewhat contradictory, but no doubt his general sympathy for the man and his movement was well known by the late 1920s. It does not seem, however, that he spoke on TWA platforms, and his unsigned pieces for the *Labour Leader* were on sport (Mendes 2002: 77; Buhle 1992: 60; James [1963] 1993: 114).

At some point James decided to write a book about Cipriani, a political biography that would illustrate through one man's struggle the nature of crown colony government and the need for self-rule. He approached Cipriani, who agreed at once and granted him several interviews, never refusing to answer questions and providing many documents as materials for the book. "He talked and I listened with my writing-pad on my knee." James "began to study the history of the islands" and collected *Hansard*, White Papers, commission reports; "my hitherto vague ideas of freedom crystallized around a political conviction: we should be free to govern ourselves." The planned biography broadened into an attack on the whole theory and practice of colonial rule and a sweeping analysis of society and politics in Trinidad, with special reference to Cipriani and the TWA. The arguments he makes against crown colony rule were fairly standard by 1932, but the book showed, as Kent Worcester notes, a recognition of the structural factors inherent in colonialism, even if it can hardly be seen as a Marxist work. James considered not so much the economic underpinnings of twentieth-century colonialism but the political and, especially, the ideological structures, notably racism and the "trusteeship" doctrine (Buhle 1992: 60; James [1963] 1993: 113–15; Worcester 1996: 23).

In an article about Cipriani (long dead) in a Trinidad newspaper in 1962, James related an anecdote that he repeated in *Beyond a Boundary*, which was published the following year. Sometime before he left Trinidad in 1932, he used to give English lessons to the French consul, who was very "intimate" with the governor and his circle. They would talk on many subjects. Once he asked James, "If the Governor arrested Captain Cipriani, what do you think would happen?" James immediately realized that his arrest must have been under discussion within the government. He replied, "The people will burn down the town," and proceeded to enlighten the consul to the fact that this had already happened—during the Water Riots of 1903 the seat of government had been burned down, during which, as James made sure to point out, the governor of the day had barely escaped being lynched by the crowd. James could see that the consul was suitably impressed. "Cipriani was never arrested and I like to believe that I had made a modest contribution to British colonial policy" (James 1962: 17; see also James [1963] 1993: 114).[7]

That James admired Cipriani is very clear from *Life*, though except perhaps for the last few pages it is not an entirely uncritical study of the man and his leadership. In the same article published in 1962, James testified to Cipriani's influence on his intellectual and political development: "He was the man who taught me that I was a West Indian. . . . Today [1962] I think that much that distinguishes my view of politics must have come from him. Not that he ever lectured to me, but that in talking to him, listening to him and reading his speeches in a concentrated manner, something came over, or was awakened in, me which I find in my very earliest writings and speeches when I began" (James 1962: 18).

In this article and again in *Beyond a Boundary*, James asserts that *Life* was a great success, that it received very good "notices and reviews" when it was sent to Trinidad (James 1962: 17; James [1963] 1993: 119). In fact the first local reviews of *Life*, written by members of his intellectual circle back home, were distinctly cool, ranging from harsh criticism to ambivalent praise.

Albert Gomes, James's friend and perhaps rival, penned a short but savage review in the *Beacon*. It was neither a life of Cipriani nor an account of British government in the West Indies, he wrote; it should have been called "Some Incidents in the Legislative Council of Trinidad and Tobago with their Colour Implications." Gomes felt, probably wrongly, that James's "colour hang-ups" had led him to write a book that was, "as a whole, formless and devoid of any real value to the student"— and pretentious as well. Overall, bad as crown colony government was, James's "method of criticism is not very significant or sound." The chapter on Cipriani and the divorce controversy came in for special abuse, as merely a "dishonest and artless attempt to whitewash his hero's mistake." On the other hand, and ironically in view of his earlier attack on James's "colour hang-ups," Gomes thought the long chapter on the color question was by far the best, with "many shrewd things": a "very entertaining essay" on the subject, though he professed not to see the link between color prejudice and the case for self-government. Gomes concluded that prejudice would always exist except in a "classless, communist" society (Gomes 1932: 5–7). There is an exquisite irony in Gomes, who would emerge in the Trinidad of the 1950s as a distinctly right-wing politician, attacking the future eminent Marxist theoretician for not calling for a communist revolution.

In the same number of the *Beacon*, Joshua Ward, a Barbadian "Negro" who had lived in Trinidad since 1918, expressed his "grievous disappointment" in *Life*. In his view James had "mauled the Englishman" rather than the "real culprits," the white creoles and the mixed-race people, for color prejudice within the nonwhite population was "more depressing and oppressive" than between the English and the rest. Anyway, he felt, such prejudice was timeless and universal and would exist under any form of government. For Ward, the real issue in Trinidad was "the cosmopolitan character of the community which threatens to swamp the negro. . . . The organization of local society does not promote political independence of action," an interesting point which is certainly not addressed in *Life*. Ward was referring to the ethnic diversity of Trinidad, in contrast to the simple white-black duality of Barbados, and especially to the large Indo-Trinidadian minority (one third of the population), which was barely even mentioned in *Life*. Like Gomes, Ward dismissed James's account of the divorce controversy as "worthless" and felt that "it taints and vitiates much of the credit that could be given to anything fairly stated" elsewhere in the book. Could the author of this chapter be the man "whose penetrating intellect has secured the esteem of all Trinidad," Ward asked; a biography must fairly give both sides, the bad and the good, of its subject (Ward 1932: 16–18).

Ralph Mentor, a writer, labor activist, and member of the *Beacon* group, provided a more balanced view in his piece on *Life* but still found it disappointing because it was close to a eulogy of Cipriani; James "tried to justify *almost* every political judgement" made by his subject, and when that was impossible, "he has attempted to palliate." But Mentor warmly praised James's analysis of Trinidad society as containing "penetrating insight" and "incontrovertible truth." However, he felt James was wrong to argue that crown colony government was responsible for race prejudice: this was due to historical factors going back to the slave trade and to "a vicious economic situation." Like the previous reviewers, Mentor felt that the chapter on the divorce affair was simply a crude effort to "put thick coats of whitewash" on Cipriani's actions, which had been full of "vagaries and absurdities." Overall while Mentor fully acknowledged that Cipriani deserved the gratitude of the people, he felt that James had not written an "impartial" account of local politics; it was the work of a partisan advocate, not that of a judge. This, of course, was to willfully misunderstand the whole point of the book! (Mentor 1932: 15–17).

Another member of Trinidad's literary circle, C. H. Archibald, writing in the magazine of James's old school, essayed an overall review of James as a writer, which was distinctly unflattering. Archibald found *Life* specifically disappointing. Granted its purpose was to expose the failings of crown colony rule and to urge the need for representative government, it would have been much better to have planned the book to do this straightforwardly instead of adopting the biography format, which (he believed) was a failure. With some justification, Archibald pointed to the "disjointedness" of the book, which lessened its effect "as a political tract." Yet he praised the masterly discussion of the race question and the quality of the writing, which he saw as typical of seasoned journalists "of international fame" (Archibald 1932: 16–19).

In addition to the reviews in the *Beacon* and the *Royalian*, both of Trinidad's daily newspapers noted the appearance of *Life* as soon as copies arrived in the colony early in September 1932.[8] It is perhaps unsurprising that the *Guardian*, organ of British official and business circles, savaged the book. Its English editor, Courtney Hitchins, headlined his review "C. L. R. James Attacks Everybody" and declared, "What was intended to be a live political bombshell to be dropped on Trinidad this week has proved to be nothing else but a harmless dud." James attacked everyone "except the very black people," Hitchins claimed, which could hardly aid the cause of self-government. Mixed-race people, those "not coal black like Mr James," received especially venomous criticism from James, according to Hitchins; "Negroes are the only people Mr James really praises," though James did concede that they are "not perfect." On Cipriani, Hitchins thought that his story had been told "without a single mistake to blemish a spotless record," while his struggles during the war and over the returned soldiers and the electricity and divorce controversies were chronicled in "tedious detail." This short, superficial review, suffused with obvious racism, contained only one valid point: that James had dismissed Indo-Trinidadians in one brief paragraph even though they constituted one third of Trinidad's population (Hitchins 1932: 2).

As we would expect, the other daily, the *Port of Spain Gazette*, provided a much more thoughtful and positive review of *Life*. This paper, the organ of the Creole elites (white and nonwhite), generally took more liberal positions on local issues; it had a long-established interest in local literature, and it was currently publishing long letters from James on his first impressions of England (James [1932] 2003). "Our Literary Critic" thought that *Life* was "the most significant and daring work which has come to our notice for some time." Though especially interesting to Trinidadians, it was "even more remarkable as a clear and reasoned exposition of the political problems in these colonies, as seen by a West Indian." The reviewer recognized that its revelation of the "truth about Crown Colony Government" would offend many: "Many people are going to be very sore at Mr James. In wielding his cudgels so vigorously, he has proven himself to be as regardless of consequences as the subject of his biography" (Our Literary Critic 1932: 13).

Though the picture of Cipriani was strongly drawn, this reviewer thought, even clearer was James's exposition of the system that Cipriani opposed; he had shown "a masterly grasp of political conditions" in Trinidad. Unusually the reviewer thought that in the section on the divorce controversy, James was "an acute observer and a constructive critic." Unusually too he claimed that James had "not enunciated any political doctrine. He has told a tale, he has presented documentary evidence, and has left the reader to make an inference." But only one inference was possible: "Crown Colony Government has outlived its usefulness in the West Indies." The author's analysis of the sectors of the Trinidad population (the first chapter of *Life*) was pronounced excellent, with the "hard knocks" generally "given in a spirit of fair-mindedness and in perfect good temper." The only "partiality" James showed, the reviewer thought, was in his analysis of the unofficial members of the legislature: he had singled out the "fair" members for scathing criticism but had "either eulogised the black member [A. H. McShine] or passed him off among a crowd" (Our Literary Critic 1932: 13).

It seems that copies of *Life* were sent to the other British Caribbean colonies and that the book was noticed in at least some of them. The *Port of Spain Gazette* reported that the *Daily Chronicle* of British Guiana had reviewed it positively: "Brilliantly written and stimulating to West Indian thought, the book deserves to be widely circulated throughout these colonies." This (unnamed) reviewer considered that the first chapter of *Life* was "the finest essay we have ever read" on the West Indian race question, dealing with each group "without bias." Overall the book was certain to enhance James's reputation in the region (*Daily Chronicle* 1932: 12).

In Barbados *Life* was reviewed by J. E. Brome in the *Barbados Advocate*. While Brome praised the fine style of "this splendid essay," he was disappointed that it provided neither a life of Cipriani nor an account of government in the West Indies, "except Mr James, as other Trinidadians do, thinks that Trinidad is the West Indies." Moreover the biographer must be a scholar and a historian, and judging by *Life*, James was neither; biography was not a proper medium for the parade of learning or for "the foul current of racial prejudice under the guise of a biographical setting." Still, Brome conceded, James was "unsurpassable" in his descriptions of the white and colored Trinidadians. Overall the book was a good effort to portray political life in a West Indian colony and suggested that James had "a bright future before him" (Brome 1932: 10).

It is interesting that the reviews by men in James's own circle in Port of Spain were, if we discount the racist piece by Hitchins, distinctly less generous than those published in the daily newspapers in Trinidad, British Guiana, and Barbados. Certainly these 1932 reviews were not especially gratifying, but perhaps for James, already moving on to other projects in England, they could be quietly forgotten.

James and West Indian Nationalism

In 1932, when James left Trinidad, his politics might be described as anticolonialist and nationalist, with a leaning toward the sort of Fabian socialism that Cipriani espoused. Of course, he was not yet a Marxist of any variety. He was also an accomplished writer who had tried his hand at several genres.[9]

It is interesting that, when his ship stopped en route for England at Barbados, James spoke to the new Forum Club of that island. It was a literary and debating society of young, nationalistic, educated Barbadians, not unlike the *Beacon* group. It is even more interesting that his talk was noticed by the Barbadian police and by the governor, who wrote to a friend in the Colonial Office about it. Informing him that James was then (he was writing in May 1932) in England staying with Constantine in Nelson, the governor concluded, "It looks at present as if these young men [James and the Forum Club members] were not deliberately worse than would-be journalists or imitation politicians." Perhaps this marks the first time that James would come under official surveillance for his political activities (Chamberlain 2010: 128, 146n22).

Both *Life* and *Case* reflect the emergence of James as an advocate of West Indian nationalism and are important early statements of the anti-colonial and self-determination movement in the Caribbean. James has described in *Beyond a Boundary* how significant Learie Constantine was in his own political thinking at this time. Constantine's insistence that "they are no better than we"—they being the British, the colonialists—provided James, as he wrote in *Beyond a Boundary*, "with a slogan and a banner. It was politics, the politics of nationalism" (James [1963] 1993: 113). In Nelson soon after his arrival in England, the two of them quickly "unearthed the politician in each other. Within five months we were supplementing each other in a working partnership which had West Indian self-government as its goal." Of course, the publication of *Case* the following year was designed to make an explicit appeal to British readers for self-government for the British Caribbean (James [1963] 1993: 110–11, 113, 115–16; see also Constantine 1933).

It can therefore be plausibly argued that James was an important early spokesman for the nationalist cause in the region. The editors of his *Party Politics in the West Indies* note that James, in *Life* and in *Case*, was making the case for self-government for black subject peoples when this was "almost unthinkable" and that his work "helped to number the days of Western colonialism." Indeed, they argue, these two publications "would establish James not only as the intellectual journalist of the West Indian political independence movement, but that of Africa as well." Another writer has made much the same claim: "His pamphleteering work in the thirties made him a founding father of the modern independence movements" in the West Indies and in Africa (Walters and Gomes 1984: ii–iii; Berman 1996: 70).

James himself, not surprisingly, made some large claims for the impact of his two publications of 1932–33 on Trinidad and the Caribbean. In the preface to *Party Politics* (1962) he simply stated that *Life* "has done its work"—meaning it had prepared the way intellectually for the successful achievement of self-government in the West Indies. In *Beyond a Boundary* he went further. Referring to the labor protests in Trinidad and elsewhere in the late 1930s, James wrote, "One Government commentator, in reviewing the causes, was kind enough to refer to the writings of C. L. R. James as helping to stir up the people. The chief of these was the Nelson publication [*Life*]. These books did more. I continually meet middle-class West Indians and students who say this: When the upheavals did take place these books were high on the list of those few that helped them to make the mental and moral transition which the new circumstances required" (James [1962] 1984: xxvii; James [1963] 1993: 121).

Such claims are difficult if not impossible to verify in any objective way, but there can be no doubt that his two political publications of 1932 and 1933 stand high among the important statements of the West Indian nationalist cause in the prewar period. But James himself, as is well known, lived abroad between 1932 and 1958. It was not until the latter year that he returned to Trinidad and made another foray into local and regional politics between 1958 and 1962. Despite the passage of twenty-six years, for James the continuities were very obvious: "Immediately I was immersed up to the eyes in 'The Case for West-Indian Self-Government.' . . . It seemed as if I were just taking up again what I had occupied myself with in the months before I left in 1932, except that what was then idea and aspiration was now out in the open and public property" (James [1963] 1993: 225).

These continuities are clear when one compares *Life* with *Party Politics*, the major piece of writing to come out of James's Trinidadian political foray of 1958–62. As Walter Look Lai notes, his analysis in the 1962 work "was a development on similar insights James had made since the 1930s" about local politics, society, and race relations, especially in *Life*. In *Party Politics* James returns to his cherished theme of the failures and absurdities of the West Indian middle classes, so salient in *Life*; indeed at one point he reproduces two paragraphs from the earlier work. His contempt for the black and mixed-race middle strata of Trinidad and the region had stayed with him; but, unlike in 1932, that class was now in power in Trinidad and Tobago and was not minded to accept such contempt and (as it could easily be seen) arrogance from the returning son (Look Lai 1992: 185–86; James [1962] 1984: 121–31).

Party Politics expresses James's disillusion with the way nationalist politics had worked out in Trinidad and his anger and hurt at the famous split between him and Eric Williams and his party in 1961. At the end of *Case* James had written an impressively prescient passage: "No one expects that these Islands will, on assuming responsibility for themselves, immediately shed racial prejudice and economic depression. No one expects that by a change of constitutions the constitution of politicians will be changed. But though they will, when the occasions arise, disappoint the people, and deceive the people and even, in so-called crises, betray the people, yet there is one thing they will never be able to do—and that is, neglect the people." In *Party Politics* James argued that in Trinidad and Tobago under Williams, the people were still marginalized and an autocratic leader—now an elected prime minister rather than a British colonial governor—still dominated politics and government: "A national flag and a national anthem and colonialism dressed up in new clothes do not make a new society." To James, "the whole politics of Independence has pushed the people back and not forward." In characteristic style he summed up: "The King is dead. Long live the King. Colonialism is dead. Long live colonialism" (James 1933: 32; James [1962] 1984: 138, 151–58, 173).

Needless to say, James's view of Williams and his party and government, as laid out in *Party Politics*, can hardly be accepted as a balanced assessment of either. But it is interesting that at the same time as he wrote that book, he also contributed an article to a Trinidadian newspaper that praised Cipriani in extravagant style as "the greatest of all British West Indian political leaders"—by implication, of course, saying that Williams was not in that league. This long article explained why he had decided to write Cipriani's biography and justified his continuing admiration for the Trinidadian (who had died in 1945). Cipriani had absolute faith in the ordinary West Indian, James wrote; "I have not seen such comparable faith in any other West Indian politician." Cipriani was always about the people's work, the mark of "politicians of the highest class," with a connection to the masses that was innate, not learned or affected. He was also a "very humane, very decent human being," and such a personality, especially in a small colonial society, would always "exercise a powerful if incalculable effect" on everyone who came into contact with him. James summed up, "As a politician he did many useful and valuable things. On the whole he left Trinidad and Tobago and the West Indies a larger, not a smaller place, than he found them. And he has expanded our conception of West Indian public personalities" (James 1962: 17–18).

Cipriani has maintained his high place in the popular historiography of Trinidad and Tobago. Writing in 1962, Eric Williams thought that he "deserves in full measure the esteem in which he has been held by large sections of the population of Trinidad." A statue of him occupies a prominent place in downtown Port of Spain, a city with very few monuments to individuals, and the nation's labor college is named for him. Though Williams's analysis of Cipriani's work in his 1962 national history is very slight, it is mainly positive: the Captain is named as the first of "the great trinity in our movement for self-government" (the others are T. U. Butler and Patrick Solomon) and praised as the one who "gave dignity to the barefooted man." Yet, Williams points out, he ended up opposing Butler and justifying World War II (Williams [1962] 1964: 220–24, 242).

In my own general history of Trinidad, first published in 1981, I noted that Cipriani was by and large defeated by the realities of crown colony government: "[His] performance in the council was not very effective in terms of achieving practical legislative reforms of real benefit to the working class." Yet his role as a legislator, I thought, "contributed significantly to the political awareness of the people," and under him TWA helped to politicize important sectors of the population, above all the urban lower middle and working classes. It was clearly the first organization to undertake mass political mobilization in Trinidad and Tobago. Of course, Cipriani's hold over the workers, at its height around 1930, declined after 1934–35—something that James did not have to deal with in *Life*, published in 1932—and by the time of the upheavals of 1937 he was clearly on the wrong side. He denounced the strikes and riots led by Butler, distanced his organization from the strikers and told the Commission of Enquiry that they had been led by those with "Communistic tendencies." No wonder that the socialist working-class leader Elma François called him, around this time, "Britain's best policeman in the colonies." Yet certainly up to 1933–34 Cipriani had contributed significantly to opening up the political arena to important segments of the population hitherto largely excluded and unorganized (Brereton 1981: 168–73, 181).

The author of the most important study of Trinidad and Tobago's political history between 1917 and 1945, Kelvin Singh, is generally harsher in his judgment of Cipriani. While noting the importance of the TWA in the 1920s and pointing out that Cipriani was the unchallenged leader and indeed idol of the workers at least up to the mid-1930s, Singh considers that his performance in the legislature was "ambivalent" and showed a tendency to compromise with the authorities even when this was not necessary. Singh questions the sincerity of his socialist beliefs and charges him with naïveté for his faith that the British Labour Party would support self-government for the colonies when in power. (Of course it did not.) Overall, Singh concludes, Cipriani's intervention in politics "was intended to contain and moderate the Black working-class challenge to the colonial power structure." The only role he could play was as mediator between the ruling class and its middle- and working-class challengers. His insistence on constitutional and nonviolent methods of protest failed the masses: only direct action, demonstrations and strikes, could bring change, methods that Cipriani consistently disavowed (Singh 1994: 125–27, 137–46, 150–57, 212, 224).[10]

Conclusion

It is fair to ask here how valuable James's two publications of 1932–33 are to readers today. Two James scholars have described *Life* as "a curious mixture of legislative excerpts, military race-relations history, almost incidental island detail, biography, and antiracist or protonationalist arguments" (Henry and Buhle 1992c: 263–64). This description is not unjust and points to the disjointed character of the book that had been noted by some of the Trinidadian reviewers in 1932. It may well be the case that James rushed to finish the manuscript before he left for England early in 1932, so that he could take a completed (nonfiction) book in order to establish himself as a serious writer there. This might partially explain its unfinished, hurried quality, especially the final section—and the promise of a "second volume," which never appeared but was intended as the conclusion to the work.

Yet it retains value as a biography, however inadequate, of Cipriani. James himself recognized its limitations, and in his 1962 article wrote that "a serious biography of such a man will add to our stature politically, socially and personally." None has appeared; James's work remains to this day the only dedicated attempt to tell Cipriani's remarkable story (James 1962: 18).

Most of *Case*, of course, reproduces material from *Life*, but it remains important as a brief but powerful polemic in favor of West Indian self-government, directed at a British readership. Its limitations as an analysis of colonialism are clear. As Worcester notes, James based his argument for self-government on the facts that there were sufficient numbers of educated people (nonwhites) in the colonies to assume the tasks of governance and that the population as a whole was essentially "Western" in culture and outlook. There was no critique of the legacies of slavery and indenture, no exposé of conditions on the plantations or in the oilfields. The stress was on the education and Western culture of the black middle class, a deeply paternalistic kind of argument that was, it seems, justly criticized by the working-class radicals of Nelson in 1932 (Worcester 1996: 24, 28).

Yet it remains an early and powerful statement of West Indian nationalism. F. S. J. Ledgister, in a recent work, sees *Case* as an important forerunner or precursor to the "Creole nationalism" that would emerge full-blown in the British Caribbean colonies after World War II. In developing and disseminating the message that West Indians were entitled and ready to govern themselves as early as 1932–33, James had produced work "of tremendous importance for Caribbean thought" (Ledgister 2010: 97).

There can be no doubt that these two works were important in James's own development as a thinker and writer. *Life* was his first book-length publication, and his first attempt, other than in fiction, to describe and analyze West Indian society and politics. Ledgister describes *Case* as "a first, untutored effort at developing a coherent political vision of the Caribbean in the modern world." The themes of colonialism and racism would resonate in all his later work; *Case* "is the work of a colonial subject who had successfully begun the decolonization of his mind" (Ledgister 2010: 97).

As several scholars have pointed out, *Life* was James's first attempt to study politics and history through the biographical method, to examine political life and theory through the lens of an individual life. This was to be a method James employed frequently in his later writings, whether the life was Constantine's, Toussaint's, Padmore's, or Nkrumah's. In this sense it can be seen as an important preparation for *Black Jacobins* and indeed for much of his later work (Henry and Buhle 1992b: 122–24; Worcester 1996: 22).

The relationship between a leader and a broad social or political movement was always a key theme for James. In 1931, reviewing Gandhi's autobiography for the *Beacon*, he wrote, "I am now more than ever inclined to believe that they [leaders] shape the environment more than the environment shapes them." He thought that Gandhi's power to mobilize the Indian masses around the principles of noncooperation and nonviolence was simply "miraculous" (James 1931b: 17–19). Around the same time, he published a long biographical essay on Michel Maxwell Philip, a mixed-race Trinidadian lawyer of the late nineteenth century, in the *Beacon*. This was a lively sketch of an interesting man, but we see James using Philip's life to illuminate Trinidad's history and to "vindicate" the island's "Creoles"— people of African or mixed African-European descent—from accusations of underachievement or lack of culture. "This sketch has been written in vain," he concluded, "if creoles do not see that Maxwell Philip's memory is to be treasured . . . because he was a man of that varied intellectual power and breadth of culture which make him and such as he the fine flower of a civilized society" (James [1931] 1999: 87–103).

James examined the relationship between a movement and its leader in *Life*, which can be seen as an important "apprentice" work in developing the methods of analysis that allowed him to examine that relationship in his later, and far more sophisticated, works with a biographical orientation. He used the biographical method as a means of historical "vindication" of people of African descent and to confront colonial and racist ideologies.[11] This is perhaps most obvious in *Black Jacobins*, dominated by the life of Toussaint L'Ouverture, but we can also see it in other works; for instance, in *Beyond a Boundary* the towering figures of W. G. Grace and Frank Worrell help to structure James's narrative and analysis. The biographical method allowed James to move between the individual and his role and agency, and the structural forces that (as a Marxist) he believed determined historical change. It reinforced for James the value of historical writing and the historical method as a tool for political analysis and practice.[12]

The Life of Captain Cipriani, first published over eighty years ago, remains of value to students of the Caribbean and of James. It was his first full-length work of nonfiction, his first foray into biography as a mode of historical and political analysis. It remains the only book-length study of the pioneering Trinidadian labor leader. The pamphlet that was spun off from the longer work was an important expression of anticolonial thought in the Anglophone Caribbean in the 1930s. As early statements of the West Indian nationalist argument, both *Life* and *Case* are of considerable historical, and historiographical, significance. As important milestones in the development of one of the region's major twentieth-century thinkers and writers, they are of great interest. And if I may be permitted to end on a personal note: when I first began my research into Trinidadian society in the late nineteenth century, I found the masterly exposition of social and race relations in that society, in the first chapter of *Life*, to be immensely valuable, not to say revelatory.[13]

Notes

I thank Robert Hill, the series editor, for asking me to write the introduction to these two works by James, and for his supportive, constructive, and patient advice during the revision process. I am also grateful to the anonymous reviewers for the Duke University Press; their comments and criticisms helped to improve the essay.
1. The two texts will be subsequently referred to as *Life* and *Case*.
2. For the British West Indian military experience during World War I, see Howe 2002; Elkins 1970.
3. A recent analysis of *Case* can be found in Ledgister 2010: 83–95.
4. A good general account of James's life in Trinidad in the period covered in this section is in Worcester 1996: 3–26.
5. See Cudjoe 2003 for an extended discussion of this tradition.
6. For the 1919–20 unrest, see Singh 1994: 14–40; Teelucksingh 2013: 45–52; Martin 1973.
7. Interestingly, while he is identified as the French consul in the 1962 article in a Trinidad paper, he is simply "the——consul" in *Beyond a Boundary*, published in Britain.
8. The TWA's organ, the *Labour Leader*, began publishing on 26 August 1922 and ceased publication on 30 January 1932, before copies of *Life* arrived in Trinidad in September 1932.

9. For evidence of his maturing skills as a writer at this time, see his 1932 letters written for the *Port of Spain Gazette* from London (James [1932] 2003).

10. Jerome Teelucksingh, in his recently published doctoral dissertation, is closer to my judgment of Cipriani than to Singh's (Teelucksingh 2013: 56–80).

11. For a brief but interesting discussion of James and the historical "vindication" of Afro-Caribbean people, see Hill 1999.

12. James's use of the biographical method, and the wider theme of biography's role in the writing of the political, social, and cultural history of the colonial and postcolonial world, is a fascinating topic that, for reasons of space, cannot be further explored here.

13. This research resulted in a University of the West Indies doctoral thesis (1973) and a book (Brereton 1979).

References

Archibald, C. H. 1932. C. L. R. James. *Royalian* 1, no. 2: 16–19.

Berman, P. 1996. The Romantic Revolutionary. *New Yorker*, 29 July: 69–71.

Brereton, B. 1977. John Jacob Thomas: An Estimate. *Journal of Caribbean History* 9, May: 22–42.

———. 1979. *Race Relations in Colonial Trinidad, 1870–1900*. Cambridge: Cambridge University Press.

———. 1981. *A History of Modern Trinidad, 1783–1963*. London: Heinemann.

Brome, J. E. 1932. Review of *The Life of Captain Cipriani. Barbados Advocate*, 8 October. Reproduced in *Port of Spain Gazette*, 13 October: 10.

Buhle, P. 1992. The Making of a Literary Life. In P. Henry and P. Buhle, eds., *C. L. R. James's Caribbean*. Durham: Duke University Press, 56–60.

Chamberlain, M. 2010. *Empire and Nation-Building in the Caribbean: Barbados, 1937–66*. Manchester: Manchester University Press.

Cobham, S. N. 2006. *Rupert Gray: A Tale in Black and White*. Edited by L. Winer. Annotations and introduction by B. Brereton, R. Cobham, M. Rimmer, and L. Winer. Kingston: University of the West Indies Press. (Orig. pub. 1907)

Constantine, L. 1933. *Cricket and I*. London: Philip Allen.

Cudjoe, S. 2003. *Beyond Boundaries: The Intellectual Tradition of Trinidad and Tobago in the Nineteenth Century*. Wellesley, Mass.: Calaloux.

Daily Chronicle (British Guiana). 1932. Review of *The Life of Captain Cipriani*, 20 September. Reproduced in *Port of Spain Gazette*, 5 October: 12.

Dhondy, F. 2001. *C. L. R. James, Cricket, the Caribbean, and World Revolution*. London: Weidenfeld and Nicolson.

Elkins, W. F. 1970. A Source of Black Nationalism in the Caribbean: The Revolt of the British West Indies Regiment at Taranto, Italy. *Science and Society* 34, no. 1: 99–103.

Fraser, P. 2008. James the Writer. *Guyana Review*, 5 November.

Gomes, A. 1932. Editorial Commentaries. *Beacon* 2, no. 5: 5–7.

Harland, S. 1931. Race Admixture. *Beacon* 1, no. 4: 25–29.

Henry, P., and P. Buhle, eds. 1992a. *C. L. R. James's Caribbean*. Durham: Duke University Press.

Henry, P., and P. Buhle. 1992b. Caliban as Deconstructionist: C. L. R. James and Post-Colonial Discourse. In P. Henry and P. Buhle, eds., *C. L. R. James's Caribbean*. Durham: Duke University Press, 111–42.

Henry, P., and P. Buhle, eds. 1992c. Editors' introduction to excerpts from *The Life of Captain Cipriani*. In P. Henry and P. Buhle, eds. 1992. *C. L. R. James's Caribbean*. Durham: Duke University Press, 263–64.

Hill, Robert A. 1999. C. L. R. James: The Myth of Western Civilization. In G. Lamming, ed., *Enterprise of the Indies*. Port of Spain: Trinidad and Tobago Institute of the West Indies, 255–59.

Hitchins, C. 1932. C. L. R. James Attacks Everybody. *Trinidad Guardian*, 11 September: 2.

Howe, Glenford. 2002. *Race, War and Nationalism: A Social History of West Indians in the First World War*. Kingston: Ian Randle.

James, C. L. R. 1931a. The Intelligence of the Negro. *Beacon* 1, no. 5: 6–10.

———. 1931b. Review of Gandhi's Autobiography. *Beacon* 1, no. 5: 17–19.

———. 1932. *The Life of Captain Cipriani: An Account of British Government in the West Indies*. Nelson, Lancashire: Coulton.

———. 1933. *The Case for West-Indian Self Government*. London: Hogarth Press.

———. 1962. Arthur Andrew Cipriani. *Sunday Guardian* (Trinidad and Tobago), Independence Supplement, 26 August: 17–18.

———. 1969. The West Indian Intellectual. In J. J. Thomas, *Froudacity*. London: New Beacon Books: 23–49.

———. 1971. *Minty Alley*. London: New Beacon Books. (Orig. pub. 1936)

———. 1984. *Party Politics in the West Indies*. Edited by R. M. Walters and P. I. Gomes. San Juan, Trinidad: Imprint Caribbean. (Orig. pub. 1962)

———. 1993. *Beyond a Boundary*. Durham: Duke University Press. (Orig. pub. 1963)

———. 1999. Michel Maxwell Philip: 1829–1888. In S. Cudjoe, ed., *Michel Maxwell Philip: A Trinidad Patriot of the 19th Century*. Wellesley, Mass.: Calaloux, 87–103. (Orig. pub. 1931)

———. 2003. *Letters from London*. Edited by N. Laughlin. Port of Spain: Prospect Press. (Orig. pub. 1932)

Ledgister, F. S. J. 2010. *Only West Indians: Creole Nationalism in the British West Indies*. Trenton, N.J.: Africa World Press.

Look Lai, W. 1992. C. L. R. James and Trinidadian Nationalism. In P. Henry and P. Buhle, eds., *C. L. R. James's Caribbean*. Durham: Duke University Press, 174–209.

Martin, T. 1973. Revolutionary Upheaval in Trinidad 1919: Views from British and American Sources. *Journal of Negro History* 58, no. 3: 313–26.

Mathurin, O. 1976. *Henry Sylvester Williams and the Origins of the Pan-African Movement, 1896–1911*. Westport, Conn.: Greenwood Press.

Mendes, A. H. 2002. *The Autobiography of Alfred H. Mendes 1897–1991*. Edited by M. Levy. Kingston: University of the West Indies Press.

Mentor, R. 1932. A Study of Mr James's Political Biography. *Beacon* 2, no. 6: 15–17.

Neptune, H. 2007. *Caliban and the Yankees: Trinidad and the United States Occupation*. Chapel Hill: University of North Carolina Press.

Our Literary Critic. 1932. The Life of Captain Cipriani. *Port of Spain Gazette*, 11 September: 13.

Ramchand, K. 1971. Introduction to C. L. R. James, *Minty Alley*. London: New Beacon Books, 5–15.

Rosenberg, L. 2007. *Nationalism and the Formation of Caribbean Literature*. New York: Palgrave Macmillan.

Sander, R. W., ed. 1978. *From Trinidad: An Anthology of Early West Indian Writing*. London: Africana.

———. 1988. *The Trinidad Awakening: West Indian Literature of the Nineteen-Thirties*. Westport, Conn.: Three Continents Press.

Singh, K. 1994. *Race and Class Struggles in a Colonial State: Trinidad, 1917–1945*. Kingston: University of the West Indies Press.

Smith, F. 2002. *Creole Recitations: John Jacob Thomas and Colonial Formation in the Late Nineteenth-Century Caribbean*. Charlottesville: University of Virginia Press.

———. 2013. Rupert Gray's Vulnerability . . . and Ours. *Small Axe* 17, no. 1: 71–83.

Teelucksingh, Jerome. 2013. *The Cost of Freedom: The Struggles of the Caribbean Working Class, 1894–1950*. Saarbrucken: Scholars Press.

Thomas, J. J. 1969a. *Froudacity: West Indian Fables Explained*. Biographical note by D. Wood. Introduction by C. L. R. James. London: New Beacon Books. (Orig. pub. 1889)

———. 1969b. *The Theory and Practice of Creole Grammar*. Introduction by G. Buscher. London: New Beacon Books. (Orig. pub. 1869)

Walters, R. M., and P. I. Gomes. 1984. Introduction to C. L. R. James, *Party Politics in the West Indies*, edited by R. M. Walters and P. I. Gomes. San Juan, Trinidad: Imprint Caribbean, i–xv.

Ward, J. 1932. One Negro to Another. *Beacon* 2, no. 5: 16–18.

Williams, E. E. 1964. *A History of the People of Trinidad and Tobago*. London: Andre Deutsch. (Orig. pub. 1962)

Worcester, K. 1992. A Victorian with the Rebel Seed: C. L. R. James and the Politics of Intellectual Engagement. In A. Hennessy, ed., *Intellectuals in the Twentieth-Century Caribbean*. London: Macmillan, 115–30.

———. 1993. C. L. R. James and the Development of a Pan-African Problematic. *Journal of Caribbean History* 27, no. 1: 54–80.

———. 1996. *C. L. R. James: A Political Biography*. Albany: State University of New York Press.

THE LIFE OF CAPTAIN CIPRIANI

An Account of British Government in the West Indies

TO LEARIE CONSTANTINE

For reasons not private but public,
and quite unconnected with cricket.

CONTENTS

FOREWORD

This is a foreword, not a preface. All that I have to say—for the present—is in the book.

I would like to thank all those who have helped me. It would be unwise, however, to mention their names.

I would welcome corrections of mistakes of fact, also any information, old or new, books, newspapers, pamphlets, official documents (particularly the Report of the Committee on Wages 1919), in fact anything which would be useful in the effort to rid ourselves of the weight we have carried so long that some of us scarcely realise that we are carrying it.

C. L. R. James.
3 Meredith Street,
Nelson, Lancs.

This book is a biography, but a political biography. It is not written for the purpose of describing the personal career and probing into the motives of Captain Cipriani. It is written as the best means of bringing before all who may be interested the political situation in the West Indies to-day. These British West Indian islands, although numbering almost a score, divide between themselves a population of not two million and an area of just over twelve thousand square miles. Yet they are among the oldest and most historic portions of the British Empire, and the time has come for the British Government to make good the promise it has always held out to colonial populations—self-government when fit for it. Of the movement for this Captain Cipriani is the leader in Trinidad and recognised as such in British Guiana and the Leeward and Windward islands. During the last eighteen years, he has been engaged in a series of struggles against the bad manners, the injustice, the tyranny, and the treachery of Crown Colony Government. This book will give a plain and documented account of these struggles. The movement seeks a change in the constitution. The remedy to be applied must be constitutional. But no survey of any constitution is of value unless it takes into consideration the different elements of the society for which the constitution functions.

The West Indian islands are British colonies and are ruled by Englishmen. First, therefore, the English.

The English at Home

The English have played a great part in the history of the world during recent centuries, and are among the most remarkable of European nations.

They are distinguished among modern peoples by their genius for politics in which on the whole they have led Europe. Geographical position, climate and historical events have helped them, but in politics they owe much to their common-sense, their capacity for tolerance, and their instinct for compromise. They are people of very good nerves and very good temper, which makes them unlikely to lose their heads in a crisis. They are possessed of an almost limitless determination, and whatever the confusion in which they find themselves, attack their difficulties, often without much over-intelligence, but with a good nature and unshaken faith in themselves which invariably brings them through in the end.

More than all civilised peoples, their political life is free from peculation. Corruption does not stalk through their politics naked and unashamed as it does, for instance, in the politics of America. Among English people the administration of justice is such as to gain the confidence and win the admiration of all who come into contact with it.

That, in fact, their honesty, is one of their chief characteristics. They are comparatively speaking, one of the most honest of peoples. Sharp as they have been in business during the nineteenth century, their men of business have never been given to fraud as the Americans or the French.

They are a snobbish people. Englishmen like to bow and scrape to their superiors only a little less than they like to be bowed and scraped to themselves. Among no people has aristocracy had so much prestige. And yet in their illogical and common-sense way they manage to combine with this as much real democracy as any other modern nation can show. Recently a chimney sweep was elected Mayor of an English town, and there is not an Englishman, whatever his political complexion, who is not secretly proud of his country as a place where such a thing is more likely to happen than in any other country in the world.

They are deeply patriotic and have a belief in themselves and their country more than perhaps any other people, though it is not paraded as it is among other nations: Britons never never shall be slaves is typically un-English. They have a great respect for law and order, and are a people as well-behaved as the Germans. Yet they have a far more independent spirit. Despite their abiding patriotism and their respect for authority, they maintain a vigour of speech and freedom in criticism which astonish strangers and entitle them to their claims that England is the home they can point to a roll of distinguished names surpassed by that of no modern people. Their standard of public service has been and remains high. But despite all these things, and the almost formidable common-sense which has helped them so much in the practical business of life, it remains true that the bulk of them, even when well-educated with the best education that their country can give, are uninterested in things of the mind and concerned with culture only as a means of personal advancement. Schopenhauer, at dinner in an inn every night, put a gold coin on his table before he began and when he was finished put it back into his pocket. The waiter was moved to ask him why. "Do you see those English officers over there?" said the philosopher, "The first night that they speak of something else besides women and horses this gold coin is yours." But the waiter never got it. They spoke of women because they were officers, but they spoke of horses because they were Englishmen. If anyone happens to meet fairly frequently any group of Englishmen even of University education he will find that as a rule they dislike civilised conversation and look with suspicion, if not positive dislike, upon anyone who introduces it into their continual reverberations over the football match, the cricket match, the hockey match or the tennis match. How often one meets an Englishman, who, though not a sportsman, tries to make it appear as if he is or has been one. Quickness of intelligence, quickness of spirit would seem to be drawbacks rather than helps to political stability. And in this respect the English are a people more akin to the early Roman than to the ancient Greeks or the modern French.

Closely allied to this lack of intellectuality is their well-known stiffness in social intercourse. With them it is almost a virtue. It has frequently been pointed out how often in their popular fiction the man of great physical strength and inability to say anything for himself usually predominates and carries off the heroine in the end. The "strong, silent man" is a fiction almost entirely English. The third charge that they think too well of themselves very probably is the natural outcome of the other two. The combination of these qualities has a consequence of great importance. Persons who have no particular interest in things apart from their practical value are not likely to welcome but more likely to resent whatever is new, whatever is strange, whatever is different, particularly when to this is added a continuing sense of their own importance. Persons for whom ordinary social intercourse is so difficult find that it requires an almost superhuman effort to be friendly with persons of different race and upbringing to themselves. That is why the French, in intellectual and social culture the most advanced people in Europe, have little or no colour prejudice, while the English, mentally inert and socially inelastic, are, despite their long experience of Empire, the most prejudiced people upon the face of the earth.

Generalisation over such a diversity of types as is necessarily included in a nation of millions of people is naturally dangerous to handle, but nevertheless the Frenchman, the Spaniard, the Chinaman are recognised types, and so is the Englishman. The portrait here given is not complete, but for our purposes it is sufficient, doing justice to the sitter from the angles which concern us most. Such, then, is the Englishman. He goes to the colonies and he carries with him both his virtues and vices. Unfortunately, the matter does not end there.

The Colonial Englishman

The Englishman who comes to the colonies, especially the smaller colonies, is of necessity neither highly placed at home nor, judged by European standards, of first-class ability. For if he were, it stands to reason that he would never leave the opportunities of living in one of the great centres of civilisation or enjoying the rewards which a great country like England can offer to those who have exceptional ability or influence.

Bourgeois at home, he finds himself after a few weeks at sea suddenly exalted into the position of being a member of a ruling class. Empire to him and most of his class, formerly but a mere word, becomes on his advent to the colonies a phrase charged with responsibilities, it is true, but bearing in its train the most delightful privileges, beneficial to his material well-being and flattering to his pride.

Being an Englishman, and therefore accustomed to think well of himself, in this new position he develops a powerful conviction of his own importance in the scheme of things, and it does not take him long to become absolutely convinced not only that he can do his work well— which he often does—but that no local man can ever hope to do the work which Englishmen are doing. Which is an entirely different thing.

Every West Indian colony produces and for many years past has produced men of outstanding ability. In the Legislative Council of Trinidad to-day the two greatest personalities are easily Captain Cipriani and Mr. L. A. P. O. Reilly, both local men, besides whom most of the officials are pigmies. And small as has been the share allotted to local men in the government and councils of the island, yet during the last two generations our best men have been consistently superior either in intellectual gifts or political strength of character to the large majority of the official class. It is not hard to see why. The exceptionally able local man, especially if he is a man of colour, stays at home. The Englishman who can match him also stays at home. In fields where the competition is open, as in medicine and law, the local man demonstrates his superiority in no uncertain fashion. Indeed, there have been periods in recent years when the weakness of the Crown lawyers in opposition to the members of the local Bar has been one of the standing jokes of the community: "You can commit murder in this country if you can pay a good lawyer. The Crown is sure to lose." To-day and at most times during the last thirty years such positions as Chief Justice, Colonial Secretary, Puisne Judge, Attorney-General, Solicitor-General and Surgeon General could be filled two or three times over by local men, most of them men of colour. And the only reason why there would be difficulty in filling some of the other positions is because on the whole coloured men of ability and ambition have kept away from engineering, agricultural science and education, knowing that the rich white men who have always controlled most of these spheres would not employ them and there was a limit in the government service beyond which they could not go. This will sound to those unacquainted with the West Indies as an exaggeration. Some of these will have in their minds savage people, speaking primitive languages, worshipping heathen gods, walking about in the sunshine, dressed to suit the climate, in fig leaves and feathers. They will be disillusioned a few pages further on.

It is not claimed here that the Englishman in the West Indies, for instance, is not capable of doing the work which he comes here to do. That would be a gross libel on many able men and a very unfair statement of the case. But the colonial Englishman can show no such superiority to local men as would be deduced from our form of government or by his monopoly of the superior positions. Every West Indian knows these things.

What is the effect on the colonial Englishman when he recognises, as he has to recognise, the intellectual strength of these men whom he is sent to govern? Men have to justify themselves, and he falls back on the "ability of the Anglo-Saxon to govern," "the trusteeship of the mother country until such time (always in the distant future) as these colonies can stand by themselves," etc., etc. He owes his place to a system, and the system thereby becomes sacred. Blackstone did not worship the corrupt constitution of England as the Colonial Office official worships the system of Crown Colony Government.

"Patriotism," says Johnson, "is the last refuge of a scoundrel." It is the first resort of the colonial Englishman. How he leaps to attention at the first bars of "God Save the King!" Empire Day, King's Birthday, days not so much neglected in England as ignored, give to the colonial Englishman an opportunity to sing the praises of the British Empire and of England, his own country, as its centre. Never does he seem to remember that the native place of the majority of those to whom he addresses his wearisome panegyrics is not England, but the colony in which they were born, in which they live, and in which they will probably die.

This excessive and vocal patriotism in an Englishman is but the natural smoke of unnatural fires burning within. That snobbishness which is so marked a characteristic of the Englishman at home, in the colonies develops into a morbid desire for the respect and homage of those over whom he rules. Uneasily conscious of the moral insecurity of his position, he is further handicapped by finding himself an aristocrat without having been trained as one. His nose for what he considers derogatory to his dignity becomes keener than a bloodhound's, which leads him into the most frightful solecisms.

In Grenada in 1931 there was a very orderly demonstration by all classes of the community against a decision of the Governor. One man who with his family had been invited to Government House for some social function took part in it. The Governor wrote him cancelling the invitation, but informing him that the cancellation did not apply to his wife and daughter who could come if they wanted to.

It is not surprising that the famous English tolerance leaves him almost entirely. At home he was distinguished for the liberality and freedom of his views. Hampden, Chatham, Fox who has so little to his credit on the Statute Book of England and yet whose memory is adored by so many Englishmen, Dunning and his famous motion: "The power of the Crown has increased, is increasing, and ought to be diminished," these are the persons and things which Englishmen undemonstrative as they are, write and speak of with a subdued but conscious pride. It is no accident, the Whig tradition in English historical writing. But in the colonies any man who speaks for his country, any man who dares to question the authority of those who rule over him, any man who tries to do for his own people what Englishmen are so proud that other Englishmen have done for theirs, immediately becomes in the eyes of the colonial Englishman a dangerous person, a wild revolutionary, a man with no respect for law and order, a person actuated by the lowest motives, a reptile to be crushed at the first opportunity. What at home is the greatest virtue becomes in the colonies the greatest crime.

The colonial Englishman, it is fair to say, retains some of the characteristics which distinguish his race at home, but he is in a false position. Each succeeding year sees local men pressing on him on every side, men whom he knows are under no illusions as to why he holds the place he does. Pressure reduces him to dodging and shifting. Thus it is that even of that honesty which is so well recognised a characteristic of the English people,—but I shall let an Englishman speak. "It is difficult," says Mr. Somervell, the historian, "for white races to preserve their moral standards in their dealings with races they regard as inferior."

Here again it is perhaps necessary to say that the generalisation is, like all other generalisations, apt to be unfair. Most coloured men have met many charming English people. The Englishman of real intellectual quality is almost wholly without the baser sort of colour prejudice. Quite a few English people come to the colonies who being of finer perceptions and more delicate sensibility than the average run of their fellows are obviously willing to take a man on his merits. But they cannot maintain their attitude. They are drawn inevitably into the circle of their own people, and find that for them to do otherwise than the Romans would be equivalent to joining a body of outsiders against their own. Thus it is that in the colonies, as wrote an English official in the West Indies "such large and intelligent classes of Englishmen come to have opinions so different from those for which the nation has ever been renowned at home."

No one questions, be it observed, the inalienable right of people to keep what company they please. To-day and as far as can be seen for many years in the future, perhaps always, men of the same race, men of the same nation, will inevitably keep together. Under some very strong common stimulus, literary or artistic, bibulous or sexual, individuals of different races will seek each other's company, but on the whole under circumstances where no strong prejudice exists against a particular race or people, the large majority of mankind prefers and probably to the end of time will continue to prefer its own people as associates. It is but natural that the Englishman official or unofficial given his antecedents should maintain the exclusiveness that he does. It is an attitude with which one can even sympathise. A man cannot change his nature. Further, to many of these colonials it must seem that they are a small island, surrounded by a sea of coloured people and in danger of being swamped should they permit the least opening of the dykes. It must be granted, too, that the behaviour of some of the coloured people is annoying in the extreme, and English people who show any inclination to friendship are pursued and badgered by people of colour, some of whom will lose all sense of proportion in their efforts to find a footing, however precarious, in English society. All these allowances may be made for the colonial English. But these can no longer be allowed, as they have done in the past, to retard the political advancement of nearly two million people.

Along with the colonial Englishman it is also necessary to bracket the white creole.

The White Creole

The white creole has a far better knowledge and understanding, instinctive and not formulated though it may be, of the coloured people among whom he has lived all his life. He has gone to the same schools with the better educated of them—there is no segregation in the West Indies—and he knows better than any official Englishman their all-round ability in everything they attempt. Still, from reasons of racial pride, he prefers to make common cause with the Englishman and combine with him to keep the great bulk of the people in subjection. Did the white creole throw his weight on the side of the people, the situation would be changed almost overnight. Not fifteen years after the British occupation—at the beginning of 1807—Trinidad was asking for some form of Representative Government. But it was the white creole and the Englishman of the unofficial class who were asking for it. In those days the vast majority of the coloured people were slaves, and those who were not were of no political importance. But with the rise of the coloured people since the emancipation of the slaves, the white creole, and, of course, the Englishman, official and unofficial, dread nothing so much as any form of Representative Government. It is not exactly an equal partnership. The Englishman sees to it that the white creole is junior partner in the firm. Not too often does he allow him the privilege of becoming a head of a department, and when he does it is usually one of the lower grades. But the white creole, especially the one who is in business, is quite satisfied, knowing that he and the official Englishman can control the Colonial Office in Downing Street. Sometimes their interests clash, as, for instance, when the Colonial Office decided that all goods bought for the local Government should be bought in England, and not from the local merchants.

"My God," said Mr. G. F. Huggins, President of the Associated Chambers of Commerce of the West Indies, "is it not painful to feel the injuries and the disregard with which one is treated at this time? . . . I appeal to the Government to pay more attention to the views expressed by those who are governed and who have something to say in just such occasions as this."

But these occasions of disagreement are rare, and usually the last thing that the white creole wants is for the British Government to pay attention to the views of those who are governed.

The white creole suffers from two disadvantages, one of which he understands, and the other of which he probably does not. The first is climate. Trinidad has seen no group of men more brilliant than the early Frenchmen who just before the British occupation and for many years afterwards helped to make this island what it is to-day. Yet their descendants are men immeasurably below them, and as a rule the white creole of any distinction has had his blood reinforced by the blood of the despised negro people. The European blood, by itself, cannot stand the climate for more than one or two generations. Here and there the second or third generation may use wealth, early acquired, to bolster mediocre abilities into some sort of importance, but the tropics, as the generations succeed each other, take a deadly toll of all those strangers from temperate climates who make their home permanently here. In one West Indian island has the white man been able to escape this physical and mental deterioration. The island of Barbados, twenty-one miles long and fourteen miles broad, is swept continually by the breezes of the Atlantic, and white men have been able to live and flourish there for many generations. Elsewhere they have had to pay for their intrusion.

The second disability of the white creole is less tangible, but perhaps more important. He finds himself born in a country where the mere fact of his being white, or at least of skin fair enough to pass as white, makes him a person of importance. Whatever he does, wherever he finds himself, he is certain of recognition. But with this power goes no responsibility. Englishmen govern the country, and all he has to do is to keep well with them, not a difficult thing to do under the circumstances. It is an atmosphere which cramps effort. There is not that urgent necessity for exceptional performance which drives on the coloured man of ambition, and the white creole suffers accordingly. But it is not a disease which is easily seen by those who suffer from it, nor is the disease, even when diagnosed, one for which the patient is likely to take the remedy. This is a defect from which the Englishman in the colonies who has grown to manhood in England does not suffer. He has come from a larger country. He has a better sense of values; usually he comes to the colonies with the very definite idea of improving his position, and thus is not affected by his superior prestige in the same way as is the ordinary white creole.

The Coloured People

We come now to the remaining section of the community, the coloured people. The bulk of the population of these West Indian Islands is coloured, over eighty per cent being negroes or persons of negroid origin. But what the stranger unacquainted with these islands must get very firmly into his head before he goes any further is that these people are not savages, they speak no other language except English, they have no other religion except Christianity, in fact, their whole outlook is that of Western civilisation modified and adapted to their particular circumstances. The negroes in the West Indies are the descendants of slaves who were carried there from the early seventeenth century until 1807, when the slave trade was stopped. The slaves had no chance of preserving language, religion or customs on any extensive scale, for in order to lessen the chances of combination and rebellion, members of the same tribe, even members of the same family, were carefully separated from each other. To-day in very remote districts there survive traces of heathenism, just as in England, France and many of the most civilised parts of the world. But in the West Indies to-day there are no native peoples in the sense that there are natives in Africa or in India. There is in these colonies to-day no conflict between freshly assimilated ideas of modern democracy and age-old habits based on tribal organisation or a caste system. This lack of tradition, this absence of background, is in one sense a serious drawback. It robs the West Indian of that national feeling which gives so much strength to democratic movements in other countries. But it has its advantages, for it robs those who would wish to deprive him of his political rights of one of the chief arguments which they flourish so glibly when speaking of other non-European peoples. But, nevertheless, the question must be squarely faced. What sort of people are these who live in the West Indies and claim their place as citizens and not as subjects of the British Empire?

It was not so long ago when the answer would have been comparatively simple. They are coloured men, and therefore, ipso facto, inferior. But to-day three hours spent in looking through the work of modern biologists would stop any intelligent man from asserting theories of race superiority, whatever he might continue to think in secret. Academic discussion does not help us here. We shall have to take the people as they are.

Now here I shall rely chiefly on the written evidence of Englishmen themselves, colonial officials, but not the average official: rather men who were responsible for the government in these parts and who had every reason for observing closely and comparing the various sections of the people whom they ruled, with one another and with Europeans at home. I shall choose three, Mr. C. S. Salmon, President of Nevis, Colonial Secretary and Administrator of the Gold Coast, Chief Commissioner of the Seychelles Islands, etc., whose book "The Caribbean Confederation" appeared late in the eighties; next Lord Olivier, a former Governor of Jamaica, whose well known book "White Capital and Coloured Labour" appeared in 1905; and finally Sir Charles Bruce, Governor of the Windward Islands, Governor of British Guiana, Colonial Secretary and afterwards Governor of Mauritius who published his reminiscences "The Broad Stone of Empire" in 1910.

The advocates of negro inferiority and the necessity for trusteeship would have you believe that the average negro is a simple, that is to say, a rather childish fellow. Compare this with Lord Olivier's opinion that:

> The African races generally have a subtle dialectical faculty, and are in some ways, far quicker in apprehension than the average Caucasian.
>
> The African whether at home, or even in exile, after the great hiatus of slavery, shows practical shrewdness and aptitude for the affairs of local government. His legal acumen is higher than that of the European.

Of his capacity of assimilation hear Mr. Salmon:

> But although the British Black Men have many faults of character this much can be fairly said for them: they have made marvellous good use of the opportunities—the very few opportunities—that have been put in their way. This is all the proof practical men want to enable them to decide whether a people are really fitted for the rights of citizens. The British Black Men having, on the whole, answered this question affirmatively, no more in fairness should be required of them.

This was written nearly fifty years ago. And yet even at that time Mr. Salmon could also say of their capacity for governing themselves:

> They are fitted for it now, that is the point. There are few people in the world who are not fitted for local self-government of some kind. The real question is not the unfitness for it but the amount of it demanded.

The trustees would have you believe that the average negro is a savage fellow bearing beneath the veneer of civilisation and his black skin, viciousness and criminality which he is losing but slowly and which only the virtual domination of the white man can keep in check. Says Lord Olivier:

> In the matter of natural good manners and civil disposition the Black People of Jamaica are very far, and, indeed, out of comparison, superior to the members of the corresponding class in England, America or North Germany. Of their alleged savagery:

This viciousness and criminality are, in fact, largely invented, imputed and exaggerated in order to support and justify the propaganda of race exclusiveness.

The last argument of the trustees even when they have to admit the extraordinary progress of the negro, is that he does not produce sufficient men of the calibre necessary for administering his own affairs. Every white man who had been in the colonies knows in his heart how true are these words of Lord Olivier's.

> ... negroes are now indisputably the equals of white men in categories in which one hundred years ago their masters would have confidently argued that they were naturally incapable of attaining equality

The white men know that, but the inevitable inference they will not draw. They keep on repeating that the negro lacks this and that and the other thing, and when they do give him a chance give him grudgingly and stand aside looking critically on waiting to jeer at his mistakes. They can no longer deny him ability, but they impugn his character. He lacks "something." Yet Sir Charles Bruce after his wide experience could say:

> In the meantime, such has been the energy and capacity of the Afro European population in the Crown Colonies, where they form the bulk of the general community, that there is no department of Government, executive, administrative, or judicial, in which they have not held the highest office with distinction, no profession of which they are not honoured members, no branch of commerce or industry in which they have not succeeded. I have illustrated in another chapter their position in the political and social system of Mauritius, and what I have said applies equally, so far as my experience goes, to their position in the West Indies.

But men do not achieve these things by being deficient in essential elements of intellect and character. It is very laborious work demonstrating the obvious, but experience has proved only too often that in this connection it has to be done.

The three men referred to all wrote over twenty years ago. The present generation is the war generation, the last twenty years have seen the

coloured people making such astonishing progress that they are over-
flowing by sheer weight of members into some hitherto closely-guarded
preserves of the official Englishman and the white Colonial. In 1931 comparing the position of the African in Africa and the African in Jamaica
the "New Statesman and Nation" wrote:

> The complete obliteration of all distinctions in the laws between
> Europeans and Africans, was resorted to only when compromises
> that would work without being partial slavery had been searched for
> in vain. In the West Indies this solution of the problem has proved
> to be the final one. In Jamaica, where with a population of a mil-
> lion the experiment has been tried on an adequate scale, there is a
> mainly African legislature and an overwhelming African electorate
> and civil service. The reason most people have no idea that this is
> so, is simply that there are never any scare headlines about Jamaica.
> There is no "unrest," no raping of white women, no lynching of
> black men. The rates of crime and pauperism are the lowest in the
> world. Five families out of six have land of their own.

And of this mainly African legislature chosen by a mainly African electorate Major Woods (now Lord Irwin), Under-Secretary of State for the
Colonies, wrote in his report after an official visit:

> What I have seen of the elected members of the Legislative Council
> of Jamaica, taken as a whole, gives me no reason to doubt the essen-
> tial sanity of the electorate in their choice of representatives. Speak-
> ing generally, the body of elected members appears to be animated
> by a high sense of public duty and a full consciousness of their re-
> sponsibilities as a partner in the business of government.

I do not want to protest too much. I think I have quoted enough. I
could have said all these things myself. I preferred to let Englishmen,
and Englishmen of the official class, say them. There are, however, a few
things which on that side of the question can still be pointed out. In the
West Indies to-day the legal and medical professions contain far more
coloured men than white. In fact, seventy-five per cent, at least of the
K.C.'s in the West Indies are coloured men. The Civil Services are over
ninety per cent coloured; newspaper reporting, elementary education
and some of secondary, all the routine and a large part of the executive

work of the majority of the business houses (except a few from which they are jealously excluded) all are done by coloured men. The superior positions are for the most part held by white men simply because those appointments are in their hands. What people do in their private businesses is their own affair. Government posts are another matter. And we shall make fitting reference later to this pernicious system of bringing strangers and shoving them into the most important positions in the Government, to the exclusion of well-qualified and competent West Indians. It is just as well to note, in passing, the curious psychology of the colonial official, who, in many cases, it is clear, quite honestly believes that he and a few others like himself are absolutely necessary to the system and were they withdrawn it would immediately topple to the ground.

It will be urged, and with justice, that there has been presented only one side of the picture. It has to be admitted that the West Indian coloured man is ungracious enough to be far from perfect. Persistently denied compulsory education, scandalously neglected by the Colonial Office after the first thirty years which followed emancipation, with first the planters and then the industrialists, not only careless of but positively hostile to the advancement of the masses of the people, with officials urged on to work by nothing else beside that tender weapon a sense of duty, it is not surprising that there is still much ignorance among the West Indian masses to-day. But should the natural leaders of the people get the opportunity that they have been asking for, that ignorance which is confined for the most part to the more remote districts would disappear in a generation. The West Indian, however, has his own particular characteristics. He lives in the tropics, and he has the particular vices of all who live there, not excluding people of European blood. In one respect, indeed, the African, or the negro in the tropics, has an overwhelming superiority to all other races—the magnificent vitality with which he overcomes the enervating influences of the climate, whenever the motive is adequate or the reward sufficient. But otherwise the West Indian people are an easy-going people. Their life is not such as to breed in them the thrift, the care, and the almost equine docility to system and regulation which is characteristic of the industrialised European. If their comparative youth as a people saves them from the cramping effects of hide-bound tradition, a useful handicap to be rid of in the swiftly changing world of to-day, yet they lack that valuable basis of education which is not so much taught or studied as breathed in from birth in a country where people have for generation after generation lived settled and orderly lives. Not nearly so dull and slow as the English they pay for it by being less continent, using the word in its widest sense, less stable, and on the whole decidedly less dependable. And this particular aspect of their character is intensified by certain social prejudices peculiar to the West Indies, and which have never been given their full value by those observers from outside who have devoted themselves to the problems of West Indian society and politics.

Those who are not West Indians think of the population of the West Indies as being composed of white and coloured, or white and black. By any strict classification the population is actually composed of a small percentage of white people, a large percentage of actually black people, and about fifteen or twenty per cent of people who are a mixture of both races. From the days of slavery, when these were born into the world, the offspring of the slave girl and the white owner, or overseer, they have always claimed superiority to the ordinary black, and a substantial majority of the more ignorant of them still do so, although how they reconcile this attitude with that of equality to the white man is beyond ordinary comprehension. With emancipation in 1833, these hybrids and their descendants soon assumed the position of a sort of middle-class between the white aristocracy and the negro masses. Before long, however, with extended opportunities, the negroes themselves established a middle class. But between the brown-skinned middle class and the black there is a continual rivalry, distrust and ill-feeling, which, skilfully played upon by the European people, poisons the life of the community. Where so many races and colours meet and mingle, the shades are naturally difficult to determine, and the resulting confusion is immense. There are the nearly white hanging on tooth and nail to the fringes of white society, and these, as is easy to understand, hate contact with the darker skin far more than some of the broader-minded whites. Then there are the browns, intermediates, who cannot by any strength of imagination pass as white but who will not go one inch towards mixing with people darker than themselves. And so on, and on, and on. Clubs are formed of brown people who will not admit into their number those too much darker than themselves, and there have been warm arguments in committee, the whole question being whether such and such a person's skin was fair enough to allow him or her to be admitted into a club without lowering the tone of the institution. Clubs have been known to accept the daughter and mother, who were fair but to refuse the father, who was black. Daughters have denied their mothers by avoiding them in public. A dark skinned brother in a fair skinned family is sometimes the subject of jeers and insults and impolite intimations that his presence is not required at the family social functions. Fair skinned girls who marry dark men are sometimes ostracised by their families and given up as lost. There have been cases of fair women who have been content to live with black men but would not marry them. Should the darker man, however, have money or position of some kind, he may aspire. Thus the brown skinned man with many thousands a year will, after effort enough, be admitted into the society of the very fair, the rich black into the society of the brown. In fact it is not too much to say that among coloured people the surest sign of a man's having arrived is the fact that he keeps company with people fairer in complexion than himself. Remember, finally, that the people most affected by this are people of the middle class who, lacking the hard contact with realities of the masses and unable to attain to the freedoms of a leisured class, are more than all types of people given to trivial divisions and sub-divisions of social rank and precedence.

Here lies, perhaps, the gravest drawback of the coloured population. It is difficult for them to meet together and combine, for it is the class that should in the natural course of things supply the leaders that is so rent and torn by these colour distinctions. As I have written in the chapter on the Legislative Council:—

> Thus it is nothing surprising to find on the Legislative Council three or four coloured men each a little different in colour who are more widely separated from one another than any of them is from a white man; and whose sole bond of unity is their mutual jealousy in their efforts to stand well with the governing officials.

In Trinidad and British Guiana there is a large East Indian population, and of this fact much is made by obstructionists. The East Indians form only about twelve per cent of the whole population of the West Indies. And although there are about thirty-three per cent of them in Trinidad, they do not form anything like a problem, being a law-abiding people, who along with their weaknesses have certain qualities of thrift and industry which make them admirable citizens. If there is no great affinity between the average negro and the average East Indian there is not the slightest trace of ill-feeling, and though the East Indians are an older race, tenacious of certain of their racial habits, yet the latest generation is as much West Indian "creole" as is the local term, than it is oriental, a tendency which is certain to increase now that East Indian immigration has been stopped. There is no communal problem in the West Indies.

Such, then, are the coloured peoples of the West Indies. They have their faults, and no attempt has been made to gloss over them. There is one thing, however, which remains to be said. And I shall let another than myself say it. It is a thing that is too often forgotten by those who discuss peoples and their relation to constitutions. Education and experience will influence, but they will not change people. The Indian is an Indian. The Chinaman is a Chinaman. The Englishman is an Englishman. The West Indian is and will always remain essentially a West Indian. When Mr. Prudhomine David, a black man, opposed in the Legislature a scheme for having nominated members on the Port of Spain Municipal Council, he stated a truth which it is well for those interested in colonial administration to bear in mind. The extract is long, but for more reasons than the one stated (though that is important enough), I quote it in full. The Director of Public Works, an Englishman, made a long and violent address in favour of Mixed Councils. Mr. David concluded his own speech:

> That address, Sir, was remarkable in many respects—in none more so than in respect of the spirit of self-satisfied superiority which it betrayed. The Hon. Member told us that there were manifold objections to a wholly elective authority, the first and greatest being that the people of Port of Spain and of the Colony generally are not yet fitted by their personal qualities, character and education to exercise such an important privilege as self-government on English lines in and later on he said that there must be some common cause why representative institutions did not thrive in the tropics where few of the people were of Anglo-Saxon descent—that it would appear that in the tropics the great mass of the people had not the energy, self-reliance and determination to be masters of their own

destinies which characterised the people of Great Britain—that 'the great mass of the people were uneducated, with few ideals and small wants beyond those which a too-bounteous nature provided with little exertion on their part.' And in developing his scheme of a mixed Council, he continued:— 'Of the elected members not much need be said beyond that they would be chosen by an electorate with a fairly low franchise: they would voice the wishes of the people, and in return they would receive and pass on to the people full explanations of the questions brought before the Council. They would see and ultimately believe that the great object of the Government is always to devise measures for the benefit of the Colony and of its whole people, and not merely a section of them, and that the Government emphatically is not such a Government as is described in the local Press.' Sir, I do not hesitate to say that these opinions concerning the people of the Colony, coming as they do from a public officer of the rank of the Director of Public Works, from a member of the Executive Council who professes also to know the mind of the Colonial Office, have done more than the volleys of the police* to alienate the people from the Government of this country, and have sealed the fate of Mixed Councils in the Colony for at least a generation. What self-respecting man will serve on a board comprising men who believe him unfitted both by character and education to represent his fellow-citizens? What self-respecting man will serve on a board upon which the functions reserved for him are 'to voice, to receive and pass on explanations, to see and ultimately to believe' while others are acting? Sir, though wanting in the determination to wrest the control of our destinies from our powerful masters, we are, nevertheless, determined not to suffer ourselves to be their dupes, and unless I am very much mistaken as to the character of my people, we shall never accept the mockery of a representative body so pertinaciously insisted on by the Director of Public Works.

It may well be that the supporters of nomination are in substantial agreement with the Hon. Director in his estimate of the people

[*He refers to the riot in 1903 when he himself was an eye-witness of the brutal shooting down of innocent people by the police.]

of the Colony, that while the Director has rashly exposed the motives by which his proposal has been prompted, the former have considered it necessary to observe that discretion of speech without which the harmony of class relationship in this country cannot be maintained. I am at a loss to understand why the Director, holding the views he has expressed of the mental and moral state of this community, should be anxious to impose on us this hybrid creation of his, and my difficulty has not been lessened by his announcement that he will probably have retired before any change in the constitution of the local authority becomes law. His own explanation is that in no other way can the voice of the man of the people become articulate. But, believing as he does that we are too indolent, ignorant and dishonest to be entrusted with the smallest share in the management of our affairs, why should he wish to defile the pure stream of administration, with, in no matter what proportion, the corrupt and ignorant elective element? According to him, thinking men have abandoned all hope of making anything but taxpayers of us dwellers in the tropics, and mixed boards in Bombay, Colombo, and other cities of the East testify as to the advent of this era of despair. In this city, as our old municipality has been totally destroyed, and, owing to ethnological considerations as it seems is never to be revived, surely no useful object would be served in inducing us to voice wishes which we are to be forever without the power to realise. I doubt not but that before this discussion is ended the Hon. Director will see that the situation does not admit of half measures; that if we are the degenerate lot that he believes us to be the Government's plain duty is to retain the administration of the town in its hands as now; while if, on the other hand, his estimate of us is merely the outcome of race antipathy and personal resentment, the pledges that from time to time have been given that the present arrangements are only temporary and will be replaced by better ones, can only be redeemed by the grant to the people of Port of Spain of the right which they formerly enjoyed, of electing their own representatives to look after their own affairs.

If that applied a generation ago, it applies to-day with greater force. These colonies have been marking time for over thirty years. The British

Government should say definitely, "We have our fingers in your neck, and we are going to keep them there," or they should do what they did with Canada nearly a hundred years ago—grant to the people the right of electing their own representatives to look after their own affairs. Despite the prophets of evil, the Port of Spain Municipality, an entirely elected body, has been a conspicuous success. The colonies are now ripe for a change. Twice during recent years, the people of Trinidad have had to send deputations to the Colonial Office protesting against the actions and attitude of the local Government. The unofficial members of the Grenada Legislative Council have walked out of the Council room, the only effective means of protest at their disposal. The unofficial members of the Dominica Council have done the same. British Guiana, for administrative purposes always considered a part of the West Indies, daily voices its discontent. It is strange that the British official, with his long experience of having to pack his traps and go from Canada, Australia, New Zealand, South Africa, Egypt and Ireland, while yet the people of India speed the parting guest, despite all this has not yet learnt to recognise when he is outstaying his welcome.

Many West Indians (and a few Englishmen too) have worked for the emancipation of the West Indies. Their story will be told in time. But none has worked like Captain Cipriani. That is why his biography is presented here. His work is at a critical stage. That is why it is presented now.

Arthur Andrew Cipriani was born on the 31st January, 1875. His father was Albert Henry Cipriani, a planter of Santa Cruz. The Ciprianis are a family of Corsican descent, closely related to the Bonaparte family. They came to Trinidad over a hundred years ago, and have their place in the history of the Island. One of them, Eugene Cipriani, made a large fortune, but the most distinguished member of the family has been the Captain's uncle, Joseph Emmanuel Cipriani. He was a solicitor and Mayor of the city of Port of Spain for seven years. He played a great part in the lighting of the city and the laying out of Tranquillity, and it is after him that the Cipriani Boulevard is named. He not only spent time on Port of Spain, but also much of his personal fortune, giving largely to charitable causes.

Captain Cipriani, one of three brothers, lost both parents early, and at six years of age was himself very nearly lost. He, his mother and his two brothers were all struck down with typhoid. Old Dr. de Boissiere passed through the rooms and examined them.

"The mother is improving," he said, "but this one (pointing to the future legislator) will die."

The boys lived and it was the mother who died. His father was already dead, and he was brought up by one of his father's sisters, a Mrs. Dick. He went to a little school carried on above the Medical Hall by a Miss Jenkins, and there he stayed until he was seven, when he left for St. Mary's College. At College with him were Gaston Johnston, the Lassalle brothers (Charlie and John), Dr. Pollonais, Napoleon Raymond, and many other good creoles. Young Cipriani played cricket well and was a good runner. The boys were not coddled in any way. They fought vigorously and often, but Father Brown, the Principal, gave them a chance, and though always willing to hear and settle when disputes did reach him, never interfered unduly. Sometimes, however, things used to go far. Where the Holy Name Convent now is there was a college for Spanish boys. St. Mary's and Queen's Royal College boys used to sit the annual examinations together in the Princes' Building, and after fighting with the questions in the hall would seek a little refreshment by joining together and making a concerted attack on the boys of the Spanish College. Some serious fights used to take place. Fists first; then stones and bottles; but when the sons of Venezuela went as far as knives the Police had to interfere and bring these inter-school events to a close.

School-life had its politics, which after all is nothing else but the art of people living well together. Now and then among the priests there were some hot-headed Irishmen who would be inclined to take advantage of the boys. But the boys kept together and stood up for their rights; and Father Brown was one who always realised that boys had rights as well as masters.

Arthur Cipriani left St. Mary's College at sixteen in the Senior class. He had not done badly, but was handicapped by an atrocious hand-writing which he preserves unimpaired to this day.

His father had trained his uncle's horses and he had grown up in racing. As soon as he left College, some of his richer relations offered to send him away to qualify as a veterinary surgeon. But his immediate family did not wish him to accept the offer, and he refused it. Already he knew horses, and he started to ride and train. He had his trainer's license at eighteen, and regularly made the round of the different racing centres, Trinidad, Barbados, British Guiana. In between he worked on the cocoa estates of his relations and friends.

He was nearly shot dead one night at "La Chaguaramas," the cocoa estate of Mr. Leon Centeno at Caroni. He was sleeping in the estate-house when he was awakened by a noise outside. He got up, opened one half of the window, and saw a man walking towards the cocoa-house. He called out to him, and the man turned and fired a revolver, the shot going through Cipriani's forearm. He still wears the scar.

The incident is still a mystery. Many people thought it was no other than Centeno himself, who was known to be a practical joker. It was believed that he had intended merely to frighten his friend, but that the shot, as revolver shots will, had taken an unexpected course. Centeno, however, originated a theory that Cipriani was not quite right in his head, and had shot himself. His theory did not find acceptance, and some time after he left the Island, to which he never returned.

For years Arthur Cipriani divided his time between racing and cocoa estates. Increasing weight made him give up riding, but he trained regularly, besides which he had and still has a passion for horse-racing. He thinks that racing in those days was of a better class than it is to-day, and there was more sport. Although the stakes were smaller, owners were very keen to win. But there was more good feeling between them then than now. They fraternised more, and successes were celebrated with big dinners and receptions. There was not so much gambling, there were no sweepstakes, but among those who went to see, much innocent enjoyment on the merry-go-rounds and swings, while among the real racing men there was not so much question of gain, as honour and distinction for the various colonies. Vigilant, Mr. José de Montbrun's horse, was one of the best of creoles. Mr. W. S. Kernahan's Ivanhoe was another great horse. Dr. Farnum also raced some splendid horses, but on the whole he thinks that no better horse than Ella Snyder ever came here.

So for twenty years he went about his business, working on estates and training horses. He became Secretary of the Breeders' Association, but though well-known in racing circles, was on the whole a rather solitary man, going about in his khaki trousers and khaki tunic open at the neck, an inconspicuous figure of no particular importance.

The course of his life seemed settled. He saw his thirty-ninth birthday, and was only a few months short of forty when in 1914 the War broke out.

The Contingents

The earnest appeal just made to you by the lecturer appeals to me, as well as to most of you who are in the hall, with a peculiar force. It is those of you who, like me, are British subjects not of English parentage, but of alien descent, and owe their protection to the British flag, that the appeal comes with greater force. It is true the Colony has offered £ 40,000 worth of cocoa, which has been accepted. Putting it at five cents per inhabitant, is that all we are going to offer in return for the protection of our homes and children which we are receiving? . . . . . I think it practicable for us to send one hundred

cavalry horses, and there can be no doubt about it that having secured a hundred horses there would soon be secured a hundred rid-
ers to go to the Front and fight side by side with the other Colonial
troops. . . . . The very best we can do is to try to attain that end, and
if we fail we will still have the satisfaction of knowing that we had
tried to do our duty.

It was his first public speech. The occasion was a lecture, "Sayings on
the War," delivered by Mr. Algernon Burkett, at St. Ann's Hall, Oxford
Street, to help the Trinidad Breeders' Association in their effort to buy a
hundred cavalry horses for the English Army. The War was not yet two
months old.

Then followed a long struggle by the people of Trinidad, led by Mr.
Cipriani and the "Port of Spain Gazette," to be allowed to play their part
in the War as members of the British Empire. At the very beginning of
the War, many felt that the services of Trinidadians should be offered to
Britain, but they had not forgotten the opposition and ridicule of the official English section in the colony to a similar proposal during the South
African War, and the curt refusal of the Home Authorities. As time passed,
however, it seemed to Mr. Cipriani that unless someone took the initiative, any chance of raising a local contingent would disappear, "a condition of things I was prepared to frustrate at all costs." He approached the
Governor of the Colony, Sir George le Hunte, with a proposal for recruiting a contingent. Sir George referred him to the Commandant of Local
Forces, Lieutenant Colonel Swain. Mr. Cipriani learnt from Colonel
Swain that the Government would not be a party to any such undertaking, that it was pledged to find a force for local defence which had already
been raised, and would not consider the raising of any other. The idea
that West Indian troops should be sent to fight for the Empire was looked
upon as absurd. Mr. Cipriani gave the Government up for the time being,
placed his views before a couple of small but representative meetings,
and was guaranteed the necessary financial aid to raise, equip and ship
a contingent.

A Colonel Ducros, through the medium of "The Times," had invited
colonials who wished to join the colours to write to him or to apply in
person. On October 24th, 1914, Mr. Cipriani cabled Colonel Ducros:
"Will you accept contingent from West Indies?" Colonel Ducros cabled

back: "Sorry, contingent fully recruited." Next day Mr. Cipriani wrote to the Colonel:

> There are many men of good physique and education in this colony and throughout the colonies who are eager and who would be proud to enlist. . . . . .
>
> We are 4,000 and some odd miles from the Old Country, and the lowest fare is £ 17 10s. A few men have left, and a few more are leaving on their own, but the majority cannot afford it. . . . . .
>
> West Indians have realised it is a fight to a finish, that not only is the existence of the Mother Country at stake, but the very Empire of which we are all proud to be a part. We should feel not only isolated but slighted if our services are declined when men are still wanted to keep the flag flying . . . . . we are bottled up here, but we are eager to get out to assist the Mother Country. If you would use your influence in getting our little lot taken into service, this colony and the West Indies will be deeply grateful.

But the West Indian contingent recruited in London had already been drafted to the London Fusiliers, and Colonel Ducros had left for the Front. It was promised, however, that the subject matter of the letter would be referred to the proper quarter.

Early in December the first batch of eleven Trinidadians at their own expense left for England to enlist. The local Government contributed nothing to the enterprise, and the concession in regard to the passage rates made by the Mail Steam Packet Company known as Royal was so small as to be almost negligible. But the send-off given to these young men was perhaps the most remarkable ever witnessed in the history of the colony, and was a very fair index of the feeling of the Trinidad people.

Mr. Cipriani next addressed a letter to Horatio Bottomley, Editor of "John Bull," asking him to make representations in the proper quarter on behalf of a West Indian contingent. Meanwhile the excitement in Trinidad was growing. Articles, extracts from other newspapers in the "Port of Spain Gazette," and letter after letter by Mr. Cipriani kept on asking directly and indirectly why Trinidad was doing nothing. By the end of June Trinidad learnt that contingents from the West Indies would be accepted by the Home Government, but the news came through an extract published in the "Port of Spain Gazette" from another colonial paper. In the course of a letter to the "Gazette." Mr. Cipriani wrote:

> May I ask why Trinidad was not the leader in this movement, considering the fact that she was the first colony to offer a contingent, an offer which was repeatedly turned down by the authorithes, and which seemed to call for their censure rather than for their approval? The moment has come when it is up to the Press of the colony to call upon the local Government to do their duty.

But when Mr. Cipriani a week later interviewed the Commandant of the Local Forces, the Commandant said that he could do nothing because he had had no instructions.

Not long after, however, the Governor in an address before the Legislative Council held out the possibilities of a West Indian contingent being raised for service at the front. Meanwhile, patriotic meetings were called, and resolutions were passed urging speedier action. Still the Government did nothing, whereupon Mr. Cipriani wrote a letter to the "Gazette," asking it to open a list for recruits. The "Port of Spain Gazette" turned its office into an unofficial recruiting station, and in two days there were well over a thousand names on its list, the first of them being Arthur A. Cipriani. Mr. Cipriani again approached His Excellency, and His Excellency again referred him to Colonel Swain. In a private interview, Colonel Swain, heartily wishing, we may well suppose, that this troublesome intruder was at the bottom of the sea, explained the attitude of the Government. It would not take the initiative, thinking it was up to those who had agitated for this contingent to do the earlier recruiting. This interview being granted on condition that nothing which took place at it would find its way into the Press, Mr. Cipriani was not in a position to make known that and the other peculiar views held by the chief of the military forces of the colony. But the thousand names on the "Gazette" list seemed to turn the scale, and after a short delay the Governor in Council named a recruiting Committee. Mr. George F. Huggins, Major A. S. Bowen and Mr. Arthur A. Cipriani, with Mr. Adam Smith as Chairman. From the very outset it was obvious that the other members of this Committee had no real sympathy with the move. However, Mr. Cipriani asked permission of the local Government, and on its being granted, convened the first public recruiting meeting in Marine Square, under the chairmanship of Dr. Prada, the Mayor of Port of Spain. No government official took any part in this meeting. But that could hardly have been expected. It could hardly have been expected for many reasons, one of which might well be indicated here. When the agitation for the public contingent was at its height, His Excellency the Governor, Sir George le Hunte, K.C.M.G., Governor and Commander-in-Chief of the Colony of Trinidad and Tobago, Vice-Admiral thereof, etc., etc., took the opportunity at an Agricultural Society meeting to make a statement of his position. He said:

> When I am asked to go to a patriotic meeting and preside and speak, it is no part of my official duty. I am always pleased to do it, as I did at Sangre Grande the other day, and I am quite willing to do the same thing over, unless people keep on holding me up to public abuse—if they do that I certainly will not do it. I shall go on doing my duty, but I shall not accept invitations to public or patriotic meetings unless I am trusted. I want that made perfectly clear. It is a matter for the public. If they wish to invite me they can, but it is for me to use my discretion in a matter that is my official duty, though it is always my pleasure to do anything to help the splendid patriotic spirit which exists in the colony now. But I must be trusted and not distrusted.

So that on the whole it was better that the Governor and his friends stayed away.

But at his recruiting meeting Arthur Cipriani spoke to the people:

> If the West Indies claims a place in the sun, we must do our duty as a unit of the British Empire. It is true that we here form the weakest link in the chain. But it is said that the weakest link is the strength of the chain. (Cheers). I am one of the people. I was born and bred in this colony, was reared in it from childhood to youth, and from youth to manhood. I have shared your sorrows and your joys, and I appeal to you to-day in the name of the King to enlist, and I do so irrespective of class, colour or creed. . . . . The game has not been played in many quarters, it is not being played now. . . . .

It was now, for Mr. George F. Huggins, a member of the recruiting Committee, was the chief mover in raising and sending to England a

Merchant's Contingent from which dark-skinned men were rigidly excluded. In Trinidad, the fairer-skinned as in some mixed communities, enjoy greater advantages and have better opportunities, and thus the Public Contingent was deprived of some of the best material available. Mr. Cipriani protested without result. But the aim had been achieved. By ten o'clock on the morning after the meeting, the first contingent of men had been recruited. In September it left for England. Mr. Cipriani helped to recruit the second contingent, the third and fourth, but then decided to go to the Front, refusing the request of Sir John Chancellor to stay and continue with recruiting work.

There was some trouble about his commission, for he was already forty. The state of his health demanded an operation. But these difficulties were successfully overcome, and on the 28th March, 1917, Lieutenant Cipriani left Trinidad for Europe in command of the third contingent.

That is how Trinidad came to send contingents to the Front, a local man and a local newspaper playing the leading parts and having to exercise as much perseverance to overcome their English masters as the soldiers had to overcome the Turks in the field. But such is a Crown Colony.

As far as Captain Cipriani is concerned, one thing more remains to be said. However casually one reads over the old speeches and the old letters, certain things leap to the eye:

> I fondly hoped that a word from our masters in Downing Street and the War Office would have had the effect of getting West Indians into line. . . . . .
>
> I think both my cable and letter were submitted to the proper authorities, and I also think (I shall spare the Censor its excision).
>
> . . . . . when our efficient colonials are overlooked and preference given to unhappy European exiles. . . . The same vigour, the same sentiments, the very phrases.

It is said that the War made Captain Cipriani. So in one sense it did, in that it gave him an opportunity. But the essential Cipriani was always there.

A detailed history of the B.W.I. Regiment in the War will be told some day. Crown Colony Governments will not interest themselves in any such thing. But it will be one of the early though minor duties of a Federated West Indies Legislature to ask for and support the production of this necessary piece of West Indies history. Little of it can be told here, but nevertheless it is imperative to give some idea of the efforts and disappointments of the Regiment, for these played a great part in the political development of Captain Cipriani.

The early battalions were handicapped from the start. Officers of the old West India Regiment who were known to have been recruited from the Sandhurst failures were drafted to the B.W.I. Regiment, and old Colonel Barchard, appointed Commanding Officer, should have been placed on the retired list long before.

Nevertheless, the first battalions in Europe started training, and although most of the men came from the islands where there was little or no tradition of military organisation and discipline, they made notable progress. In November they were inspected by General Sir Leslie Rundle, who reported that he was impressed by their smart and soldier-like appearance.

It was thought, however, that the climate of England and Europe was not best suited to men from the tropics. Egypt was threatened with invasion, and it was therefore decided to send the B.W.I. battalions there for training and service. They landed in Egypt in February, and not long afterwards encamped just outside the village of Mex, a spot which was destined to develop shortly afterwards into the biggest ammunition dump in Egypt, covering many acres of land, and supplying munitions to His Majesty's Forces throughout the entire Eastern campaign. The

B.W.I.R. supplied a permanent guard over this ammunition dump during the rest of the war, and no single accident due either to negligence or inefficiency ever took place at any time. By the middle of July, 1916, the War Office ordered the Third and Fourth Battalions back to France to be used as ammunition carriers. Lieutenant-Colonel Wood-Hill, the Commander of the Egyptian Battalions, attended a conference of officers of the Egyptian Expeditionary Force to discuss the future of the Regiment. The conference put it on record that the good work done by the First and Second Battalions had been noted, they were universally well spoken of, and the conference agreed to do all in its power to get fair play for the West Indians. It was agreed also that these Battalions should be moved forward and allowed to take a more active part in the proceedings in Egypt. Colonel Wood-Hill pointed out that using the Third and Fourth Battalions in France more or less as labour battalions was doing untold harm throughout the West Indies, and that considerable dissatisfaction existed among the First and Second because they had completed a period of training and their work chiefly consisted of guards, fatigues and other garrison duties with no immediate prospect of active service. The conference decided to ask the War Office to drop the idea that the role of these men should simply be to carry ammunition and do the general work of labour battalions.

But when the news of this conference and of the suggestions that all B.W.I. Battalions should be concentrated in Egypt was made known to the various Commanding Officers of the B.W.I. Battalions serving in France, the latter, after holding a conference among themselves, sent a letter to the War Office, protesting against the suggestion that the officers, N.C.O.'s and men of their battalions objected to carrying shells. The men, they said, were perfectly happy, and on no account wished to return to Egypt. The War Office was thus confronted with the Egyptian Army Headquarters asking for all B.W.I.R. Battalions to be sent out to Egypt, and with certain senior B.W.I.R. officers asking to be allowed to remain in France. This want of unanimity on the part of the commanding officers practically killed the B.W.I. Regiment. The War Office finally decided that the First, Second and Fifth Battalions should be kept in Egypt, that no further reinforcement should be sent there, and that all successive contingents raised in the West Indies should be sent to France for ammunition work. As soon as there were enough B.W.I. shell carriers in France, the later battalions were turned into labour battalions pure and simple. In 1917 further efforts were made to try to get the War Office to allow some of these men to fight. The Commanding Officers were informed that the War Office considered the fighting qualities of the West Indians doubtful and preferred to use them on shell-carrying and labour duties. It was the old story of the black man being first refused an opportunity to be afterwards condemned for incapacity. And yet one would have thought that most of the officials who were in a position of authority over the Colonials would have been familiar with the achievements of native troops in Africa, with all the odds of modern engineering against them, and would also have read Sir Charles Dilke's account of his journey round the world, and the opinion of one of the most famous of the Confederate leaders, on the fighting qualities of the negroes during the Civil War.

On the 30th April, 1917, Captain Cipriani arrived with his contingent to find that the B.W.I.R., having volunteered for active service, had been a year with the Egyptian Expeditionary Force and had never been given an opportunity to show what it was worth in the field.

In June the Regiment received its baptism of fire from hostile aircraft, and the behaviour of the men was such as to elicit the warmest praise of the higher command. This unexpected coolness under fire may have helped the cause, for a few weeks after General Allenby gave Colonel Wood-Hill permission to attach the Machine Gun detachment of the First Battalion B.W.I. to a Machine Gun Company of the 162nd Brigade for a period of intensive training actually in the Front Line. The further use of those B.W.I. battalions depended to a great extent on the behaviour of this machine gun section under fire in the Front Line. A raid was decided upon an enemy position known as Umbrella Hill, and in this raid the B.W.I. Detachment was to take part. Three days before the raid, a new gun outfit consisting of the latest pattern Vickers Maxim replacing the old patterned machine guns was issued to the detachment.

The raid was completely successful, and the officer commanding the Machine Gun Company reported on the work of the B.W.I. gunners as follows: —

The men worked exceedingly well, displayed the qualifications necessary for a machine gun section, viz., a keen coolness in their fire and an intelligent application of what was required of them and the necessary ability to carry it out under difficulties. Although they were only issued with Vickers guns a few days before the raid, their immediate action was excellent, and they were able to keep their guns in action during a severe test.

Major-General Hare, commanding the 54th Division, reported:

The machine gun section of the First Battalion B.W.I. have taken part in the last two raids on Umbrella Hill, and both the Brigadier and the officer commanding the machine gun company with which they have been working are full of their praise. They were under heavy shell fire both times, and behaved splendidly.

The whole battalion was moved further up toward the Front Line position, and stayed there two months. It had little to do, but three men won military medals, and when the battalion returned to the lines of communication Brigadier-General V. G. Armstrong sent the following letter:

I am directed by the Corps Commander to express great regret at parting with the Battalion under your command, which since the formation of the 21st Army Corps has been attached to it as Corps Infantry Battalion.

During the operations of the last two months it has shown an excellent spirit, and the duties assigned to it have been carried out very much to the Corps Commanders satisfaction. The soldierly bearing and the smart turn out of the Battalion have been maintained under the most trying circumstances. And the fact that this applies also to detachments away from your supervision is most creditable to all ranks.

The Corps Commander wishes you and all ranks of the 1st B.W.I.R. 'good luck,' and should circumstances permit would welcome a return of the Battalion to the 21st Army Corps.

He desires that the Battalion may be made acquainted with the terms of this memorandum

Sgd. V. St. G. Armstrong, Brigadier-General,
D.A., G.M.G., 21st Army Corps.

But still the Regiment could not get the chance it wanted.

To get to the Front was impossible, and Captain Cipriani devoted himself to guarding the interests of the men who formed the Regiment. They were black, and some (though not all) of the West Indian officers, in typical creole and Crown Colony fashion, dissociated themselves from taking any active part in defence of those whom they commanded.

On account of their colour, objections were taken to their participating in the general life of the Egyptian Expeditionary Force, which contained units from every part of the British Empire, including South Africa. That the B.W.I., in cricket, aquatics and athletics, won nearly everything they competed for, did not help to improve the situation. But Colonel A. Wilson, the commanding officer, a first-class Englishman, would allow no discrimination against his regiment. Whenever any slight was brought to his notice, Colonel Wilson was prepared if necessary to interview Head Quarters, which he frequently did, and as a result the regiment was never barred.

But in Egypt it was with Colonel Wood-Hill that Captain Cipriani clashed most often. All through his period of command he did every-thing in his power to advance the interests of the Regiment by getting it into the fighting line. But he was an autocrat of the first water, had pecu-liar ideas of discipline, and went so far as to strike the men under his com-mand. Finally, Captain Cipriani reported him to General Allenby for an offence committed against Sergeant Brown, and Wood-Hill was severely reprimanded.

"Had it not been for your long service," said Allenby, "I would have broken you."

From his defence of B.W.I. soldiers at Courts Martial, Captain Cipri-ani's reputation spread, and he was at various times Prisoner's Friend for members of all units stationed in Egypt. He found himself up against the peculiar system of evidence being taken by the Adjutant who was also the prosecutor. Another abuse of far too frequent occurrence was the ex-pression of opinion from General Head Quarters on a case pending trial. Captain Cipriani served not only as Prisoner's Friend, but often as a member of the Court, and not unfrequently as member of the Court he would receive instructions from General Head Quarters that they were desirous of securing a conviction in that particular case. Often, however, Captain Cipriani found other members of the Court who would pay no attention to such unfair directions and would agree to decide the case strictly on its merits.

Once during the time of the Egyptian unrest, General Head Quarters issued an order that any soldier losing his rifle was to be tried by Court Martial for having lost his rifle by neglect. Head Quarters showed anxiety to secure convictions, as B.W.J. men were suspected of selling their rifles to Egyptian agitators. In reply to this order the Commanding Officer made the following suggestions:—

(*a*) That the men be given permission to secure their rifles around the tent pole with a padlock at nights.

(*b*) That after the Last Post all rifles be stacked in the Quartermaster's store.

(*c*) That the road running on the boundary of the B.W.I. camp, which was an open one, should be barred to traffic after dark, or that the B.W.I. be allowed an armed guard on the road.

All these were refused, with the result that natives crept into the open camp in the dead of night and stole six rifles. This was reported to Head Quarters, who ordered that all the men concerned should be immediately tried by Court Martial. The Adjutant was sympathetic and disinclined to press the charge, but the President of the Court, with his recommendation from Head Quarters that they desired a conviction, was out to convict at all costs, and convict he did, sentencing each man to six months imprisonment with hard labour. Captain Cipriani for the defence immediately sent in a petition to General Allenby, asking for an interview. The interview was granted, the case was put, and the General ordered the release and reinstatement of the men, who had already spent four days in the military prison. Similar cases cropped up from time to time, until the President of this court was changed and his place taken by an Australian. On the first occasion on which Captain Cipriani appeared before him, he put it to the President that in these cases no neglect could be proved. The President agreed and sent in a protest to Head Quarters declaring that he would not convict on any such charge. No more rifle cases were taken up.

Such was the chief occupation of Captain Cipriani at the Front. As one of the older officers in the B.W.I.R., he had no chance of fighting, because the authorities would not give the B.W.I.R. a chance to get into the line, and he was too small a man to jockey Head Quarters as he had jockeyed the local Government in the matter of recruiting. The War, however, was not destined to end without the B.W.I.R. getting at least one chance. Officers and men had almost given up hope, when late in 1918 the Australians, always very friendly and sympathetic to the West Indians, said that they would take them to the Front Line. It was at Damieh that the black men got their first chance.

A part of the First Battalion and Major Harragin charged up the Damieh Hill sides, driving the Turks from this entrenched position and capturing two hundred prisoners and seven machine guns. The First Battalion proper, supported by The Auckland Rifles, went into action in artillery formation with the same calm as if they had been on ordinary parade, and in spite of being subjected to heavy fire in the early stages of the advance, never faltered for a single moment. Driven from Chalk and Barker Hills, the Turks made for the Damieh Bridge-head, where the First Battalion Lewis Gunners opened such a terrific fire that not a single Turk succeeded in crossing. Baffled here, the Turks made their last turn for the Es Salt Hills, and the battle resolved itself into a chase.

The Turkish Army, in full flight, made its way home by the Es Salt Hills, 3,000 feet up, and over goat tracks. The B.W.I.R., without any rest and with little food and water, followed hotly in the hope of coming up with some of them again at Amman, where the Divisional Commander had promised them another scrap. After a few hours rest, a forced march through the night brought them to Amman just too late, as the Australians had already captured the village. This was their first and as it turned out their only piece of real fighting. But the work of the B.W.I.R. was a revelation to General Head Quarters. On the day following the battle, Allenby called in person on the B.W.I. wounded in the hospital at Jerusalem and thanked them for their good work. Recognition by a personal visit from the great soldier was a very great compliment, and one which will always be remembered by officers and men.

Two months later the War was over. The B.W.I.R. was given as much leave and as many facilities for visiting the Holy Land and other places of interest as was possible, and the thought of speedy demobilisation and early return home gave a new spirit to the Regiment. Unfortunately, unrest broke out in Egypt. Leave was cancelled, and demobilisation stopped, a severe disappointment to every unit in Egypt. But it gave the B.W.I.R. a chance to put another good mark to its credit, for during the long six months that demobilisation was suspended the West Indian soldiers gave less trouble and cause for anxiety than any other unit in command, carrying out their duties as guards, pickets and escorts, duties at times very irksome and including much overwork, without any trouble or fuss. By June, 1919, the unrest was quieted, and the Regiment left for Taranto in Italy, where they had been ordered for demobilisation. There it was they met General Carey Bernard, the South African, with whom Captain Cipriani was soon engaged in some of his hardest fights for the B.W.I.R. abroad.

As soon as the First Detachment arrived, though Front Line troops, they were given the job of washing dirty linen and cleaning latrines, which has been specially laid down as the work of labour battalions. The men asked that they should be marched back to Major Harragin, their Officer Commanding. Major Harragin made some enquiries, and then told the men that they had to carry out the fatigue, which they accordingly did. When General Carey Bernard heard that the West Indian soldiers had at first refused to carry out the command, he called out Major Harragin and the party. In the presence of junior officers, he directed that Major Harragin's command should be taken up by a junior, and demanded from the Major the names of the ring-leaders in order that they should be tried for mutiny. Major Harragin replied that, as all the men had refused the fatigue in the first instance, all were equally liable, and thus there were no ring-leaders. The names of the men were then put in a hat, some were drawn out, and the owners of these were tried by Court Martial and convicted, sentences ranging from fifteen months to three years being imposed.

When Major Thursfield, having taken over command from Colonel Wilson, arrived at Taranto on June 8th, he was given a letter from Brigadier-General Carey Bernard addressed to all officers commanding the B.W.I. unit, directing that no Company Commander was to deal with any case, that neither C.B. nor forfeiture of pay was to be awarded, and that field punishment was to be given for every offence. Next morning Major Thursfield paid a visit to General Carey Bernard in person. Let Major Thursfield give in his own words an account of this visit:

In the course of the interview he said that there had been trouble with men of the B.W.I. Regiment refusing to work when sent on working-parties, and directed that any similar case was to be sent for Court Martial. I told him that I did not anticipate any such behaviour on the part of my men, whose discipline throughout all the heavy duties during the Egyptian riots and on board the transport had been excellent. As, however, I had heard that the former trouble in Taranto had been caused by the men having been sent to do work of a degrading character (in one ease cleaning out latrines belonging to the Italian Labour Corps), I told the Base Gommandant that on the formation of the Regiment and on enlistment the men had been promised that they should be treated as British troops, that this promise had in Egypt always been scrupulously kept, and that I took it that work would not be given to them which British troops would not be called on to do.

He replied that he was perfectly aware of the promise, and intended to take no notice of it: that the men were only niggers, and that no such treatment should ever have been promised to them; that they were better fed and treated than any nigger had a right to expect; that he would force them to do it.

No work of this character was given to my men while I was in Taranto: but B.W.I. troops were forbidden to go into canteens used by British troops, they were not allowed to go to the cinemas when British troops were there, they were sent to a native Labour Hospital instead of the hospital for British troops, and in every way the men of the British West Indies Regiment were treated, not as British troops, but as if they were of the same status as the native labourer from the Fijian Islands.

Captain Cipriani's experience as member of the Court and Prisoner's Friend in Egypt had sharpened him and given him a thorough grounding in Army Regulations. Luckily, for the next few weeks were a series of pitched battles against tyranny, edged by race prejudice.

On a certain occasion Captain Cipriani received information that sports would be held for all regiments stationed at the base. Later, however, an officer came to him:—

"The General says that the B.W.I.R. will have their sports by themselves."

"They will do no such thing."

"But the General says—"

"I do not care what the General says."

"But he—"

"Tell him that I, Cipriani, say that the men will not take part in the sports except on equal terms with the others. "King's Regulations lay it down that there must be no discrimination, and I will see to it that there is no discrimination in regard to the B.W.I."

The officer went away, and returned.

"The General says that perhaps it would be better if you did not take part at all."

"As he likes. We prefer to keep out altogether rather than take part on the terms that he proposes."

The sports took place without the B.W.I.R. But the General himself entered in some of the swimming races, and won two or three.

Nero, the Emperor of Rome, once visited his subjects, the Greeks, and competed in their Olympic Games. The tactful Greeks allowed him to win, whereupon the overjoyed Nero let them off their taxes. How the General came to win is, of course, a matter on which it is impossible to give any definite opinion, but when the news came to the B.W.I.R. the men, sore at the way they had been treated, complimented, not the prowess of the General, but the wisdom of his competitors, and one of them allowed himself to be heard saying in public, "Oh, they let him win to make him feel happy."

As soon as this came to Carey Bernard's ears, he ordered a Court Martial on a charge of "conduct to the prejudice of the good order and discipline of His Majesty's Army," a charge usually laid against soldiers marked out for punishment, but against whom it is difficult to get anything specific.

Captain Cipriani, of course, appeared for the defendant, and walked into the Court that morning without a single note, but with his copy of King's Regulations in his hand. After the preliminaries, he raised the first point.

"I beg to submit that the Court is not properly constituted."

"What do you mean?"

"King's Regulations state that the Court is not properly constituted when a junior officer of the same regiment is called upon to sit with his senior officers as President. And on this ground I object to the Court Martial as constituted."

The trial had to be put off until the next day. Next morning of course the prisoner was convicted.

"I appeal against the decision," said Captain Cipriani.

There was some demur.

"I appeal," insisted the Captain. "King's Regulations allow me to appeal and to send the matter up to General Head Quarters."

The appeal had to be allowed, both the Court and the General fuming. Next day Captain Cipriani appeared and asked for a copy of the notes of evidence.

"King's Regulations say that I must have a copy of the notes of evidence on payment of five shillings. Here are my five shillings."

But before the matter went any further the prisoner was called up before the General.

"Now, look here," he said, "I am not going to be hard on you this time. I am going to give you a chance, but if I hear any more of this sort of thing from you again, you will pay dearly for it. Go away."

Often Court Martials' findings were quashed upon petition, on occasion even without petition, so viciously unjust were some of them. Sometimes, too, vigorous defence saved a few. But many suffered.

The reign of terror ended at last, however, and by the end of 1919 the men of the B.W.I.R., including Captain Cipriani, were all safely home again.

To Captain Cipriani the failure of the B.W.I. to get a chance until so late in the War had been a bitter disappointment. He resented the imputation on the fighting qualities of West Indians, which he felt sure the first opportunity would wipe away. The nightmare at Taranto was, of course, fresh in the mind of every B.W.I. officer and man who had passed through it, but nevertheless the men had been well treated in Egypt, where they had made for themselves a great reputation. The congratulations and good wishes came in from every side, and long after the War were still coming.

Colonel Wood-Hill, their Commanding Officer, wrote:—

I, as Commanding Officer of one of these Battalions, can only say, that having been in action with them, and having commanded the same Battalion for two and a half years. I could not wish for a finer or better set of N.C.O.'s and men, and I am proud to have associated with them. West Indians, like all other races, have their own peculiarities: they may be a little bit harder to instil discipline into, but with firmness and fact they are easy to handle, and they are extremely loyal. They possess guts, without which no man can be turned into a soldier. They are specially quick at picking up the Lewis Gun, Bombing and the hundred and one things a modern soldier is supposed to know.

Wrote Major-General E. W. Chaytor:—

Outside my own Division there are no troops I would sooner have with me than the B.W.I., who have won the highest opinion of all who have been with them during our operations here.

Lieutenant General Sir E. S. Bulfin, G.C.V.B., C.V.O.:—

I am sorry that the First Battalion had moved from my corps, while I was on leave in England, over to the Jordan Valley, and that I was thus deprived of the pleasure of commanding them in the final operation. I am very proud to hear of their successes with the Anzac Mounted Division, and always knew and was fully convinced that the regiment would acquit itself in accordance with the best traditions of the British Army.

The finest tribute was the article by Major the Revd. W. J. Bensley, D.S.O., who spent three years with the B.W.I.R. It appeared in the West India Committee Circular of June 12th, 1919:—

I am glad to have the opportunity of writing a few words about my impressions of three years in the British West Indian Regiment. . . . . .

In those early days at Seaford one very soon realised the keenness of the men to learn, the very high standard of intellect and education among the N.C.O.'s, the splendid loyalty of all to the Empire, and their impatient desire to show it as soon as possible by active work in the field.

. . . . . For various reasons, the authorities did not realise for a very long time what splendid fighting qualities the West Indians possessed. We who lived with them and worked with them knew it quite well. There is no doubt whatever in my mind that first-class fighting material was for nearly two years practically wasted, simply because no one in sufficient authority in high quarters knew anything about us. . . . . As it is, I think that our men can go back to their homes satisfied that they have not only done what they were asked to do well, but have earned for their nation a reputation which will not be forgotten. . . . .

I have said little, I find, in the way of criticism, and I don't propose to say more than a few words. Long spells of comparative idleness or of work which does not appear to be essential, are sure to have a demoralising effect on any community, and I do not think that this inevitable effect was more noticeable among West Indians than among other Tropics. . . . .

Acknowledged, as they are now, to be good fighting men, with a first-class Commanding Officer, Officers and N.C.O.'s well above the average, they are a Unit any General may be proud to have under his Command.

No one appreciated these tributes more than Captain Cipriani. He had had faith in the local black men, and the local black men agricultural labourer, shoemaker, and tailor, when placed alongside Englishman, Scotsman, Irishman, Australian, New Zealander, and South African, had held their own. They in their turn brought back to Trinidad, along with the memory of their experiences, an unshakeable affection for and confidence in the man who had stood by them so firmly. It was in Egypt and in Italy that was laid the foundation of the mutual confidence which is so powerful a factor in our political life to-day, confidence in Captain Cipriani as an unselfish and fearless leader, confidence in the masses as a people worthy to be led. He knows, in politics, as in war, that West Indians, to achieve anything, must be given a chance.

Immediately on their return home, Captain Cipriani and Major Thursfield made a concentrated effort to get the War Office to take note of the injustices that the Regiment had suffered at Taranto, and to get some of the wrongs righted. In this matter Thursfield, although a colonial Englishman, was as eager as Captain Cipriani, to whom he wrote: "I hope you do not intend to throw up the matter in disgust as this is just what they hope you will do." And later, "I am full of hope that my letter may result in something being done in Commissiong's [*sic*] case. Take my advice and have a couple of similar cases sent in. There is no hurry. We are still comparatively young and can keep our old age green with this gentle employment."

But Captain Cipriani was the last man to need any encouragement of the kind. He and Major Thursfield wrote to the War Office; Captain Cipriani wrote to Horatio Bottomley, hoping that he would be sufficiently interested to ask questions in the House of Commons. In a few cases their attempts were successful, and the findings of certain Courts Martial were reversed, but the War Office dismissed the charges of discrimination, well authenticated as they were.

There is no wish here to leave a picture in two colours only, black and white, but even granted merely for argument's sake that there is much to be said on both sides of every question, nothing can justify the disadvantages and, at Taranto, the injustices from which the B.W.I.R. suffered. Much of this account is based on documents supplied by Captain Cipriani, but there is other evidence of the substantial truth of what has been written here. No one would accuse Sir Algernon E. Aspinall, Chairman of the West India Committee, of any wish to make trouble. Yet this is his view, expressed in a letter to Captain Cipriani:—

> Thank you for your letter of the 18th instant, from which I note that you are still in Taranto. I understand, however, that there is every prospect of your moving in the near future, and I expect that you will be uncommonly pleased to get away.
>
> The letter to which you refer is a striking indictment, and I have confirmation from several sources.
>
> Wood-Hill lunched with me recently, and I had the opportunity of discussing the matter with him. It is really deplorable that so little interest should have been taken in the British West Indian Contingent.

Yet to a West Indian the most striking feature of this wretched business was not the reluctance of the War Office to use the B.W.I.R., nor the behaviour of a stray South African General, but the attitude of the local Government. Never once did it give any sign that it had any interest in what happened to the men who had gone to fight. Of efforts to help the Regiment in its struggle to get into the Front Line, the Regiment heard nothing. Captain Cipriani's complaints to the War Office had to go through the Trinidad Government, and in acknowledgment of two letters, Mr. T. A. Vans Best, the Colonial Secretary, wrote:—

> You will no doubt remember that the Colonial Government has no locus standi in connection with the B.W.I. Regiment while serving outside the Colony.

The smug complacency is too thick. Through that could never penetrate any glimmer of the truth that it is the business of any government to watch zealously over the interests of those for whom it is responsible, especially when they have left their country in the cause that these men did. The Government, as is the way of local Governments, had no interest, and as is also the way of local Governments, did not trouble to disguise the fact.

So it has been, so it is, and so it always will be until the day that these colonies govern themselves.

CHAPTER IV | Captain Cipriani and
the Labour Movement

Captain Cipriani was back in Trinidad in 1919. Before the end of the year he had started his post-war public career by accepting the post of President of the Trinidad Workingmen's Association.

This Association had been founded in the last decade of the nineteenth century, the leading spirit being Mr. Alfred Richards, now an Alderman of the City of Port of Spain. It led a chequered existence, and in 1906 had but 223 members. By 1914 it had fizzled out. But 1919 was a time when new things were being born, and old things were being reborn. The Workingmen's Association was resuscitated, chiefly through the efforts of Mr. W. Howard Bishop, now dead, who became in time Editor of the "Labour Leader," the organ of the Association. With him were Fred Adams, Julian Braithwaite, R. Braithwaite, D. Headley and W. Samuel, most of them merchants in a small way or men in business, but all coloured men and interested in their own people.

Captain Cipriani was not one of the original group, but early in the life of the new Association he was asked to become President, and accepted.

If there is anything which can prove the fitness of the people of Trinidad for self-government it is the progress of this resuscitated Association during the thirteen years since it has been restarted.

When Captain Cipriani became President in 1919, the Association functioned only in the City of Port of Spain. By 1928 there were forty-two affiliated sections in other parts of the island, besides six others distributed among the various classes of workers in Port of Spain. In January, 1930, replying to a call from Tobago, Captain Cipriani and half-a-dozen other colleagues proceeded to the island-ward and there established thirteen sections. To-day the Association has ninety-eight sections comprising thousands of members. Each section manages its own affairs, appoints its own officers, and keeps its own funds. Delegates meet once a quarter to discuss matters of general policy. To-day, as in 1919, the public meetings of the Association are assisted by plain-clothes officers busy taking notes, and doubtless the Government would rejoice to get hold of something seditious. But though Captain Cipriani gives these amateur reporters a lot to take down, they get little to carry away. Meanwhile, the frequent rallies of different sections, the questions which they discuss, Captain Cipriani's visits to section after section explaining to them matters of policy, the circulation of the "Labour Leader" until Mr. Bishop died a year or two ago, all this has made the agricultural labourers and the artisans, the masses of the people, alive to politics as at no other time in the history of Trinidad. Where formerly those who wished no change in the constitution urged the apathy of the labouring classes and their lack of interest in politics, to-day they use other arguments. The Association has been responsible directly or indirectly for shorter hours of employment in many branches of labour, particularly in wine and provision shops; for preventing employers paying wages to employees in liquor establishments; for the establishment of an Agricultural Bank; and for the introduction of Workmen's Compensation Laws. This, the introduction of a limited Workmen's Compensation Law, has on the whole been the most stimulating achievement of the Association so far. Since the introduction of this piece of legislation the working-people have received as compensation for injuries and deaths many thousands of pounds. Of the seven elected members of Council, four are supporters of the Association. At present the Association has as its chief aim the right to form Trade Unions, and, of far more importance, self-government. Perhaps the story of the eight-hour day and Trade Union agitation will show why this is so, besides at the same time revealing local labour conditions and the typical methods of a Crown Colony Government.

The Eight-Hour Day

As far back as 1922, the Workingmen's Association had interviewed Major Wood about the introduction into Trinidad of labour legislation. Major Wood replied that it was a matter for the local Government. But he might as well have said that it was not a matter for the local Government, for all the notice the local Government took of what he said.

In 1925, however, Trinidad, as a result of the Wood Commission, was granted the privilege of electing seven members on the local legislature. Captain Cipriani stood for Port of Spain, and in spite of the chief newspapers being against him, and the very strong propaganda of a powerful section, he won a remarkable victory, being head of the poll in every ward. In his first session he moved for legislation to limit the regular hours of labour in the Colony to eight per day. The Government could not accept a motion worded in so definite a form. But after a lengthy debate a Committee was appointed to "enquire whether it is desirable to introduce legislation to fix or restrict the hours of labour in any particular trade, business or industry in the Colony." The Committee consisted of the Director of Public Works as Chairman, the Protector of Immigrants, Mr. George T. Huggins (the biggest employer of labour in Trinidad), Mr. A. Fraser, head of the Trinidad Trading Co., another large firm doing different kinds of business, Mr. A. V. Stollmeyer, merchant and owner of large estates, Mr. L. A. P. O'Reilly, Trinidad's foremost lawyer and the most brilliant political figure in the Colony to-day, and Captain Cipriani. If ever a Committee looked safe, that Committee did. Excepting Mr. O'Reilly, all the members of the Committee were white men, and, excepting Captain Cipriani, all were what are usually called capitalists.

The Committee lost Mr. Huggins early in the proceedings:

> Mr. Cipriani: I propose to ask him whether he knows of child labour and whether he considers the children employed in the gangs are below fourteen years of age.
>
> Chairman: No reference will be made in the Report.
>
> Mr. Huggins: Is it suggested that we are a Committee to sit on child labour? It may be useful to posterity if we enquired into wages at the same time if you are going to proceed on those lines. This question is not included in the terms of reference, and I think it would be a pity to go outside them.
>
> Chairman: I do not think we shall be. We are not going to consider all that has been said with regard to child labour, so I do not see that there is any particular harm in hearing what these people have to say.
>
> Mr. Huggins: But we are here to consider the question of the hours of labour.

Chairman: If we are going to have objections . . . . .

Mr. Huggins: The only straight way we should go on is: keeping to the terms of reference.

Chairman: The majority of the Committee thought differently.

Mr. Huggins: Every Committee is bound by its terms of reference. Otherwise we might go into anything.

Lt. Col. de Boissiere: It is Mr. O'Reilly's particular point.

Chairman: I cannot see that there is any objection. Mr. Taylor, do you know if there are any children in the paragrass gangs?

Mr. Huggins: I protest against our going outside our terms of reference.

Mr. Taylor: Yes, there are.

Mr. Cipriani: And that the majority working in those gangs are below the age of fourteen?

Mr. Taylor: Yes.

Mr. Cipriani: How many children, in your opinion, are employed by the Usine St. Madelene, in those gangs?

Mr. Taylor: Hundreds.

Mr. Cipriani: Would you say a thousand or more than a thousand?

Mr. Taylor: About a thousand.

Mr. Huggins: Mr. Chairman. I protest. I refuse to sit. (Mr. Huggins then left the Committee).

The Committee called many witnesses who laid bare facts which had long been common knowledge among the people.

Chairman: During crop time how many hours do you get off for sleeping at home?

Mr. A. I cannot answer for all the estates, but the best days are Saturdays and Sundays.

Chairman: But during the week?

Mr. A.: In between we may get three or four hours in two nights.

Chairman: You mean three or four hours for each of two nights?

Mr. A.: Yes.

Chairman: How long does the crop last?

Mr. A.: Four months.

Chairman: Then at the end of four months you must be very ill?

Mr. A.: Very exhausted physically.

Chairman: You have been carrying on for four months with just three hours sleep every night?

Mr. A.: In order to live, we have to get through.

But some of the other workers were little better off.

Chairman: The men who bag sugar relieve each other in turn. How many hours do you think they actually work?

Mr. F.: They only get one hour off for breakfast.

Chairman: Do they get time off for dinner?

Mr. F.: Sometimes.

Mr. O'Reilly: When do they sleep?

Mr. F.: Sometimes they do not get away. Some scarcely get home at all.

Mr. O'Reilly: But they must sleep some times?

Mr. F.: They rest on the bags lying around.

Mr. O'Reilly: You do not go home during the week?

Mr. F.: Occasionally. Sometimes for three hours. Sometimes when I get off at 10 I have to get out at 2 for 50 cents.

And of the children in the fields.

Mr. Cipriani: How is the paragrass gang made up?

Mr. F.: By children from seven upwards. Some can hardly carry their baskets in their hands.

Mr. Cipriani: How many hours do they work?

Mr. F.: Nine. They start usually at 6-30 a.m., and finish at 5, having one hour off. During crop they work from 5 or 6 a.m. to 6 p.m. They do all sorts of work, helping to load carts, leading oxen, etc.

Mr. Cipriani: Artificial manure, too?

Mr. F.: That is another gang.

Mr. Cipriani: Composed of children?

Mr. F.: Yes.

Mr. Cipriani: And the froghopper gang?

Mr. F.: They are of the same size.

Mr. Cipriani: Are they large or small gangs?

Mr. F.: Between 35 and 40.

Mr. O'Reilly: Do they ever go to school?

Mr. F.: Some don't. The majority are Indians. There are a few creoles among them of about ten years of age.

Mr. O'Reilly: How many are there under fourteen?

Mr. F.: There are several gangs of children under fourteen.

Mr. Abidh, a government school-master in the estate district, gave evidence:

Mr. Cipriani: Will you tell us, Mr. Abidh, what you know of the work done by paragrass and other gangs on sugar estates where child labour is employed?

Mr. A.: In the district in which I live there are many labouring people, and they live about me. I have known them to leave their homes at 4 a.m. and not return until 7 p.m. 70 per cent. of the children who work in the paragrass gangs are from nine to twelve years of age. . . . . . During crop time they work from about 6 or 6-30 a.m., and break off at 5 p.m., and when we have a twilight they are made to work later than 5 p.m. 70 per cent. of those who go to school leave it and work in the paragrass gang, although they are of schoolable age. When these boys leave the gangs, they find themselves in gambling dens, become thieves, and are without morals and character. . . . Then 30 per cent. of the people who work in the paragrass gangs are decrepit people who are not useful for any other work. The children who work in the gangs become contaminated with the atmosphere of these decrepit people, . . . Children of this decisive age are employed in these paragrass gangs, earning from 8 to 15 cents The most pay a child of twelve years will earn will be about 15 cents a day.

Mr. O'Reilly: Of what sugar estate are you speaking?

Mr. A.: Woodford Lodge and Caroni.

Mr. Cipriani: I take it that that is your experience generally of all estates.

Mr. A.: Yes.

Col. de Boissière: You are a schoolmaster, so speak with authority?

Mr. A.: Yes.

Col. de Boissière: Should we find any of these gangs if we went to the fields now?

Mr. A.: Oh yes. I must tell you that these paragrass gangs are "colleges of vice."

Some of the employers gave evidence. Among them were Mr. Carl de Verteuil, representing the Cocoa Planters' Association, Mr. E. A.

Robinson, one of the wealthiest men on the island and a great employer of labour, and Mr. Knox, another large employer in the sugar industry.

Mr. de Verteuil's point of view was simple to grasp. Representing the Cocoa Planters' Association, he said that he had never heard one complaint from labourers, and everybody was perfectly satisfied.

Mr. Robinson and Mr. Knox looked at labour from a different angle.

> Mr. O'Reilly: Do you think it is satisfactory to have a child of ten working that number of hours?
>
> Mr. R.: This is an agricultural country. Unless you put the children on to working in the fields when they are young, you will never get them to do so later. If you want to turn all these people into a lot of clerks, cane-weighers, and people of that sort, all you have to do is to prevent them working in the fields until they are sixteen years old; then will I guarantee you will have but very few labourers in the Colony; but if you train them to work in the fields you will never have any difficulty.
>
> Mr. O'Reilly: You agree that the present system shuts them off from education?
>
> Mr. R.: They are well-fed.
>
> Mr. O'Reilly: I am talking of their education. If they are educated, they won't want to be labourers?
>
> Mr. R.: No. Give them some education in the way of reading and writing, but no more. Even then I would say educate only the bright ones; not the whole mass. If you do educate the whole mass of the agricultural population, you will be deliberately ruining the country.

And Mr. Knox:

> Mr. O'Reilly: Do you think it is satisfactory to employ children under twelve?
>
> Mr. K.: What are you going to do with them?
>
> Mr. O'Reilly: Send them to school.
>
> Mr. K.: They prefer to work in the fields.
>
> Mr. O'Reilly: You suggest that a child should go to work before ten?
>
> Mr. K.: They should go as soon as they are able to work, as long as this is an agricultural country.

Mr. O'Reilly: A child at ten would not get very proficient, even be-fore twelve, in the normal way, so don't you think it would be more satisfactory to say that a child under twelve should be sent to school?

Mr. K.: It would be of no use to them.

Mr. O'Reilly: Then they are to be without any education at all?

Mr. K.: As long as this is an agricultural country . . .

And later—

Mr. K.: Of what use will education be to them if they had it?

If the Committee did nothing else, at least it revealed the mentality of the average local employer of labour. These men were obviously still living in the days of the Game-Laws and the early factories. Between them and a modern employer, like Colonel Hickling of the Apex Co., who does show some sense of responsibility to his employees, there is a century of difference.

The evidence was conclusive, and except for Mr. Huggins, the Com-mittee sent in a unanimous report.—The hours of labour of certain clerks should be restricted to forty-five hours per week, of artisans and labourers in industrial pursuits to forty-eight hours per week. This should not apply to intermittent workers, such as domestic servants, nor to workers on sugar-factories during the period of the year when sugar was being manufactured.

It was the very last thing the Government had expected.

Faced with this unexpected difficulty, the Government acted stu-pidly, the Government acted in bad faith, the immemorial association we in this colony have grown to associate with Crown Colony Govern-ment. Granted that the Government did not wish to accept the recom-mendations of the Committee. That in itself is no crime, has happened before, and will happen again. But the Government simply put the re-port down and left it there, though it knew that this was no routine piece of legislation, but a matter in which many thousands of people were vitally interested. Captain Cipriani waited. The Government did nothing. At last, eighteen months after the report had been sent in, he moved that effect be given to the recommendations of the Commit-tee, and on the 9th December, 1927, the Legislative Council debated the question.

Captain Cipriani spoke on his motion, and when he was finished there was not much left of Mr. Huggins's minority report. He was followed by Mr. Kelshall, the elected member for Victoria, supporting the motion. Then came the turn of the Government. Mr. Wilfred Jackson, Colonial Secretary, now Sir Wilfred Jackson, Governor of Mauritius, explained the objections of the Government.

The first was that:

> . . . . . statute interferes with the freedom of contract between an employer and an employee, which is an undesirable thing to do if you can avoid it.

The second:

> . . . . . it imposes on industry a very great burden. It imposes the burden of Government supervision, regulation and inspection. The Government made such laws, the Government must carry them out. . . . . From experience I feel perfectly confident that in any attempt at a wholesale application of such principle, even in a relatively small community such as this, comparatively elaborate machinery of inspection and enforcement will be necessary, the burden of which will fall on the industry.

And the third objection was:

> . . . . . the extreme rigidity of the method. Statutory Law cannot be departed from, and that is why the method of agreement and organisation is in every way greatly preferable. It is infinitely more elastic; it is brought about by men within the trade or industry themselves, who know the conditions, reasons, variations and the hundred and one details which may make departure from the strict letter of the arrangement necessary at some particular time . . . . . If every single small exception or seasonable variation means that the employer or employee has to go running to a Government department to get a permit for this or that, it would mean an intolerable burden on industry. . . . .

In the Colonial Secretary's second objection there was nothing at all. That employers have to bear the burden of Government inspection is nobody's fault but their own: labour legislation and government inspection have always gone side by side, and there is no reason why Trinidad employers should be exempt. In fact, the evidence taken by the Committee showed that inspection of some kind was badly needed. But the rest of the Colonial Secretary's speech was an able statement of the Government's point of view, which was a very sound point of view. If the man and master can arrange it between themselves, it is wiser to avoid government interference. That was the method in England. The Government, therefore, used the official vote (all government officers) and threw out the motion, the Director of Public Works and the Protector of Immigrants sitting mute and perforce voting against the very report they had signed.

The Government had refused to introduce legislation. Make your own terms, it said. So Captain Cipriani asked the Government to introduce Trade Union Legislation. The Government refused, saying shortly that it saw no need for the introduction of Trade Union Legislation into Trinidad.

The Workingmen's Association has therefore realised, as indeed it should have done long ago, that under the present system there is nothing to be had from the Government. It neither helps the people nor allows them to help themselves. The Government must know that unless there are Trade Unions, any bargaining between employer and employee is out of the question. But it says No. It sees no reason. . . . .

Dr. Seagar, of the Imperial College of Tropical Agriculture recently conducted an investigation into the health of the labourers of Trinidad. Part of his report ran as follows.

A very large percentage of labourers over thirty showed marked heart and blood vessel deterioration, which is so marked by forty as to handicap them seriously and shorten their expectation of life.

What chance has the average labourer under such conditions and subject to such employers as the evidence of the Commission shows? When Cipriani asked the Government if they had noted Dr. Seagar's report, the Government replied in effect: Yes, it had, but what the devil did he expect it to do about it?

Not only does it leave the people unprotected in the hands of rapacious employers. It allows, if it does not encourage, the employer class to arm itself, ready to put down any industrial unrest with a ruthless hand.

In 1930, when the military vote came up, Captain Cipriani explained the system to the Governor:

..... I will only refer Your Excellency to the Civil List, and there Your Excellency will find the 2nd Battalion Trinidad Light Infantry Volunteers. This 2nd Battalion is comprised of 26 or 28 officers. There are no privates in this little army. It is a battalion of employers; a battalion made up of prominent cocoa planters and sugar planters. All of them are well-known gentlemen, and white men; and these men have been formed into that band for the purpose of quelling any attempt at industrial unrest. They have been given the privilege to use arms and ammunition without any licence being paid on these arms. Since 1919 they have been enjoying (not to say abusing) the privilege afforded them. Those gentlemen who form that 2nd Battalion—I don't suppose Your Excellency has been let into this secret yet—are known as the "Vigilantes," and those "Vigilantes" are for the purpose of being called out to put down industrial unrest, or, more simply put, a collective bargaining of Labour for a living wage. If tomorrow Labour bargained for a right wage, or attempted to bargain, or argued with their employers, the "Vigilantes" would be called out. .....

And immediately after, Mr. O'Reilly:

I feel, Sir, very much with my honourable and gallant friend the member for Port of Spain. .....

..... I do say this, that it is well understood by the community at large that our Volunteer Force is there primarily for the purpose of quelling internal disorder. This may not be admitted by the Government, but the man in the street, the first man to whom one would speak here (I do not care who he is), if he is asked the question and gives an honest reply, would say so.

That, then, is the position to-day. The Trinidad Workingmen's Association knows that it has to cut its cards straight or pay heavily. But daily it increases in membership. It has started banks in various parts of the country to keep the people out of the hands of the usurers. One of them at Sangre Grande did £3,000 business during a recent half-year. Far from getting any encouragement for this piece of work, the little bank had to undergo a lynx-eyed inspection from a police officer, and when it tried to deposit money in one of the bigger banks in Port of Spain, the money was refused. In San Fernando the Association has organised a Mutual Poor Relief Society.

The Association is affiliated to the British Labour Party and the Labour and Socialist International, and is registered at the League of Nations Bureau in Geneva. During the past few years it has been represented at the Biennial Empire Conference of the British Labour Party. Leaders and members are full of confidence and full of hope. It is not surprising. Those who can look back at what has been accomplished in a dozen years can scarcely be expected to feel uncertain of the future.

[Since the above has been written, the news has suddenly come to Trinidad as a fall from the skies that Trade Union Legislation will be introduced. The Draft Bill has already been published. What has happened in our industrial world between 1927, when the Government saw no need whatever for any Trade Union Legislation, and to-day, to cause this sudden change of policy no one can tell. The probable reason is, of course, that the Government, having the hornet's nest of divorce around its head and startled by the strength of the impulse towards self-government, now seeks to distract or delay the working classes from the main objective by throwing apples on the path. But concessions so obviously extorted do not have any placating effect.]

The Officials

The official section, composed mainly of heads of departments, comprise a solid block of Englishmen with a few white creoles generally from some other colony, because, says the Government, among other things, local men do not get that respect from their colleagues which they ought to have. Thus these officials are for the most part strangers to the community which they govern. While on every occasion one hears of the necessity of considering those who have a stake in the colony these have none except their salaries. After the Governor, the Colonial Secretary and the Attorney General are the most important members of the Government. In Trinidad there have been five Attorneys-General during the last twelve years. The position of these officials is secure, and their promotion depends not on the people over whom they rule, but on a Colonial Office thousands of miles away. It is not difficult to imagine their general bureaucratic attitude. Often they are bored to tears in the Legislature, sitting, as they do, day after day doing nothing. Unless a department comes up specially, most of the Government work is done by the Colonial Secretary, the Attorney-General, and to a lesser degree the Treasurer. Sometimes for a whole session many members never speak. There have been official members of the Trinidad Legislature who for consecutive meetings over a period of years have said nothing, but have sat in the Council, wasting their own time and the time of the public. Not only are they bored but do not hesitate to show it. There is a further unreality, because the Government can always win when it wants to. Whenever the Governor wishes, he can instruct the officials all to vote in the same way. And the Council becomes farcical when, as has been elsewhere noted, two members of a committee appointed by the Governor receive instructions to vote against their own recommendations. It is merely necessary to think of the great change which would come over English politics if the present holders of administrative positions were themselves the judges of their own actions, assured that they would remain where they were, getting automatic increases of salary until pension time or promotion to some other country. Yet that is exactly the position of the Government officials in Trinidad to-day. Here to-day and gone to-morrow, they are always wholly out of touch and generally partly out of sympathy with the coloured people who form the majority of the population. They are Englishmen as a general rule, and Colonial Englishmen at that, so that their opportuities for social intercourse, in any case small, become smaller still. These heads of departments mix almost entirely in clubs and social gatherings with the more wealthy element of the white creoles, whose interests lie with the maintenance of all the authority and privileges of the officials against the political advancement of the coloured people. Sometimes their children intermarry with the white creoles; their sons and daughters get employment in the big business houses. For all practical purposes, and indeed by the very nature of the circumstances, it is impossible that these officials who form the largest single group on the Legislature should do otherwise than support the white commercial classes and the unofficial Englishmen. "We represent large interests," said the Attorney-General in a recent debate, and every Trinidadian knows the interests he and the other officials represent. The local Government is the Chamber of Commerce, and the Chamber of Commerce is the local Government. It is difficult to state this without giving the impression of a vast conspiracy of officials and business men to oppress, and cheat the legitimate aspirations of the local people. But it works out to that. There have been and are among these heads of departments men who mean well. But, however well they mean, the system is against them. Whatever it may be in theory, in actual fact these heads of departments on the Council represent to-day nothing but the other white people in the Colony, perhaps about three per cent. Bad as this is in a colony where the population is divided into whites and native tribes, it is intolerable in a West Indian community, where in language, education, religion and outlook, the population is essentially Western.

The Unofficial Members

The unofficial members form the second group, and have always been pointed out by supporters of the constitution as forming a sort of balance to the official side. Since 1925, they have consisted of six members nominated by the Governor and seven members elected by the people. Formerly the Governor nearly always appointed white men representing business interests. He might as well have appointed a few more heads of departments for all the representation the people got from them.

But it has been the policy of the Government for some years past to appoint a few men of colour to these positions. These have usually been men of fair, and not of dark skin. And their position on the Council, and their behaviour there, give so clear an indication of certain important aspects of political life in Trinidad, that it is necessary to understand them thoroughly. For that type of man, whether on the Council or in the other departments of government, is often a more dangerous opponent of the masses of the people than the Europeans themselves.

In its broader aspect this is no new thing in politics. There is first of all the natural gravitation of all men towards the sources of power and authority. The English aristocrats of the eighteenth and early nineteenth centuries helped to maintain their power by incorporating into their system all brilliant men outside of it who were likely to prove formidable leaders of the people. Even of Disraeli, Prime Minister and Earl of Beaconsfield, the Tories could say that he was a hired professional, "the gentleman of England and a Player, given." To-day the Labour Party in England knows only too well one of its chief perils is the absorption of its leaders into the Conservative atmosphere, and perhaps—who knows—into the Conservative Party.

Again, Trinidad is a small island, and for those who have to make their way in the community or who have children or relatives to place, the two easiest avenues of success are the help of the Government or the help of the white people. A lawyer, for instance, who made himself too conspicuous fighting for his own people against white domination would naturally lose the little chance he had of gaining large fees from the great business houses which are for the most part owned by white people. Who criticised the Government too severely could hardly ask them afterwards to give his son or his friend an appointment. There is even the possibility of a nominated member losing his own place, for the Governor can appoint whom he likes. It is easy for him then to take the line of least resistance, and thus comfort himself by the reflection that after all in such a legislature he can achieve nothing that the Government sets its mind against.

There is yet another consideration no less powerful than the foregoing. These West Indian colonies offer especially to those no longer young little in the way of organised amusement, and individuals are thrown back almost entirely on themselves for recreation. The white people are the richer people, and naturally form what for the sake of a better term may be called the local aristocracy. This society is on the whole of no particular value, containing as it does little of the element of real culture. Successful grocers, commission agents, small professional men and the like do not in any part of the world constitute the elements of a truly cultured society which from the days of the Greeks to our own is of importance only for what it is and not for what it has.

Mr. Julian Huxley, after four months extensive travel in Africa, could write:

> Of a large and important section of white people in Africa, officials as well as settlers, it is not unfair to say that "The Tatler," "Punch," a few magazines, detective stories and second-rate romantic novels represent their intellectual and cultural level.

The case in Trinidad is precisely the same, and indeed the shallowness, the self-sufficiency and the provincialism of English Colonial society has long been a bye-word among cultivated persons. But they keep themselves to themselves, and thereby become exclusive. They are the wealthiest classes, they live in the best houses, have the best clubs, organise the best amusements. For the fair skinned man who does not seek much, that society seems a paradise.

But when that is said, though much is said, all is not said. There is first of all the Governor. There have been recent Governors here whom the people despised, and rightly. Of one and his entourage in particular it could be said that he represented the butler, his wife the housekeeper, and his A.D.C. the groom. But his Majesty's Representative is sometimes a man of parts, his wife sometimes a person of elegance. And whatever qualities they may have are naturally enhanced by the ". . . power, pre-eminence, and all the large effects that troop with majesty."

Now and then among the officials one finds a really brilliant man, although not often, because brilliant men would stay at home, and even if they do come out, quickly pass on elsewhere to occupy the highest positions in more important colonies. Of late, members of the Consular Body and some of the professors from the Imperial College of Tropical Agriculture have contributed their fair share to local society. Distinguished visitors often lend both tone and colour to the social dullness of local life. Any unusual social talent of local origin, once it is white, will usually find its way to the top. Thus around the Governor centre a few small groups which, though they will vary in value from time to time, yet whatever they are, are by far the best that the island can show; for the coloured people, though possessing in themselves the elements of a society of same cultural value (their range of choice being so much wider), are so divided among themselves on questions of colour, based on varying shades of lightness or darkness, that they have been unable to form any truly representative social group or groups. The result is that many a man conscious of powers above the average, and feeling himself entitled to move in the best society the island affords, spends most of his leisure time and a small fortune in trying to get as near to the magic centre as possible, in itself a not too mean nor contemptible ambition. The serious flaw in the position of the local man of colour is this, that those to whose society and good graces he aspires are not only Englishmen, but Englishmen in the colonies, and therefore constitutionally incapable of admitting into their society on equal terms persons of colour, however gifted or however highly placed (unless very rich). The aspirant usually achieves only a part of his aim. The utmost sacrifice of money, influence, and dignity usually gains him but a precarious position on the outer fringes of the society which he hopes to penetrate, and he is reduced to consorting with those fairer than himself, whose cupidity is greater than their pride. Others who feel themselves above this place at any price policy stand on their dignity and remain at home, splendidly isolated. Thus it is nothing surprising to find on the Legislative Council three or four coloured men, each a little different in colour, who are more widely separated from one another than any of them is from a white man, and whose sole bond of unity is their mutual jealousy in their efforts to stand well with the governing officials.

These matters would not concern us here except for their unfortunate reaction on the political life of the community.

Nominations to the council and government appointments are in the hands of the Government, and the Government can to-day, [and usually does,] point to the number of coloured men it has appointed. But either by accident or design it rarely appoints black men. The career of these fair-skinned men, from their point of view (perhaps also from the point of view of the Government) seems to depend to a large extent on the way, whether openly or covertly, they dissociate themselves from their own people. They have been nominated or selected for high office chiefly because along with their ability or lack of it they have shown a willingness and capacity to please their rulers. But those same arts a place did gain must it maintain. The result is that a more or less intelligent and aspiring minority occupy a position in which they do much harm and no good, for to the Colonial Office and the ordinary observer, being men of colour, they represent the coloured people, while the Government and the white creole know that when it comes to a crisis, these their henchmen are more royalist than the King. Some people have endeavoured to see in this a fatal weakness of the coloured people and a grave reflection on their capacity for leadership. It is not so. Disinterested service actuated by nothing more than a sense of responsibility to one's own best convictions is a thing rare among all nations and by necessity of less frequent occurrence in a small community of limited opportunities. These men are not so much inherently weak as products of the social system in which they live. Still, whatever the cause of their conduct, its effect is disastrous. Particularly as the Government will appoint a dark man to a position of importance only when it cannot get a fair-skinned man.

And it is indeed strange that the Government has never seen that the best man to represent the dark people is a dark man, not from any superior virtue (heaven forbid that I should talk such nonsense), but because a dark-skinned man masquerading as any sort of European naturally makes himself ridiculous. There are and always will be a few who wish to forget their own people, others who are out only for what they can get, and a few evil-minded enough to combine in their unfortunate selves both these qualities. But that is inevitable. It remains true that the darker the man, the more likely he is to feel the interests he represents on council or in government. The Government can give no reason for their persistent neglect of dark men at all. It is not because there have not been dark men of ability. Far from it. But what dark men have had to put up with can best be seen from the case of Mr. Prudhomme David, who has been quoted in Chaper I. He was, without a doubt, the most brilliant Trinidadian of the last fifty years, a distinguished lawyer, a free and powerful speaker, a man of wide culture, fearless, and of the highest personal integrity. The extract quoted is sufficient evidence of his quality. Yet when he was appointed (through the agency of Mr. Hugh Clifford, then Colonial Secretary), planter after planter on the Legislative Council stood up and said that he had no objection to Mr. David personally, but that in

The Elected Members

There remain the elected members. But Trinidad has had only two elections, and secondly the constitution is so weighted against them that they can do little. It takes a man of the courage and strength of Captain Cipriani to hurl himself continuously against the solid phalanx arrayed against him. But these elected members have not proved entirely satisfactory from the point of view of the people. That highly civilised old creature Voltaire wrote to Rousseau, the philospher of back to nature, that he had walked upright so long that it was impossible for him now to go down on all-fours. Some of these elected members have gone on all-fours so long that they are now unable to hold themselves upright. Trained in the old nominated school, their aspirations are the same, and their methods consequently the same. Some of them could be translated into nominated members without the slightest change in their attitude. For many of the things Captain Cipriani stands for and for which one would naturally expect support from elected members, he stands alone. But should some English head of department be put down for an increase of salary, one sees these elected members on their feet. "Never was such an officer, never was one so deserving. I beg to congratulate the honourable member." It is clear from their continual complimentary references to every member of the Government who happens to come up for discussion, where their real interests lie. Some of the heads of departments are able men and do their work well, but in no part of the world, even where ministers come and go by their achievements, are all men who fill administrative positions satisfactory. Of this one it is known in Trinidad that he is certainly the laziest official who has ever filled an important position in the Colony. Of another, that his subordinates are agreed that the first step towards improving his department would be to abolish his post and divide his almost nominal duties among the other members of the staff. A third exceeds his votes with a regularity that would have caused his colleagues in a Cabinet to drop him overboard long ago. But of all these things, although some of these elected members must know them as well as anybody else, they take no notice. Government, good or bad, goes serenely on. Of effective criticism the Colony gets none from them. The people are not deceived. The difficulty lies in the constitution. A man must be either resident in his constituency or have property in it amounting to £5,000. It is particularly unfair because the Government once tried this system of nominating members for constituencies and had to give it up. To-day, of their six nominated members, four are from Port of Spain. But the people who should have every facility are to a large extent robbed of real freedom of choice. Still, on the whole they do their best. In certain cases they have put persons on the Legislature who have not the qualifications in ability and character to be there. But the people are justified. They are handicapped by the system, and prefer to vote for those who will represent them badly than for those who will not represent them at all.

That, then, is the unofficial side. There remains now only the Governor in the chair.

The Governor in the Chair

At first sight it may seem that the Governor in the Chair occupies a merely formal position, but on closer observation it becomes immediately obvious that his position there is as potent for misgovernment as the other two elements of Crown Colony Legislature. The Governor of a Crown Colony is three things. He is the representative of His Majesty the King, as the Governor-General of South Africa or Australia is the representative of the King; and as such must have all the homage and respect due to his exalted position. But the Governor is also the officer responsible for the proper administration of the government. The Governor General of South Africa, like the other Governors-General, is not responsible for the government of the country. The responsible person is the Prime Minister of those countries. In Trinidad the Governor is Governor-General and Prime Minister in one. But that makes only two. The Governor has still another official position. When he sits in the Legislative Council he is Chairman of that body. The unfortunate result is that when a member of the Council rises to speak he is addressing at one and the same time an incomprehensible personage, three in one and one in three. A member of the House of Commons can pay all due respect to His Majesty the King, submit himself to the proper authority of the Speaker of the House, and yet express himself in uncompromising terms about any aspect of the Government policy which appears to him to deserve such censure. In a Crown Colony Legislature that is impossible. There is no attempt here to impugn the good faith of Governors as a whole or any particular Governor, and in temper and in outlook the Governor is usually much the best type of man. But the Governor, being responsible for the administration, is liable for criticism directed against his subordinates. It is natural that he would, it is inconceivable that he would do otherwise than defend those on whom he depends and who assist him in carrying on the affairs of the Colony. Take the case referred to elsewhere in this book, where the Government had sent a despatch which undoubtedly gave the impression to the Colonial Office that the Port of Spain City Council was insolvent and therefore was not justified in its attempt to take over the electric lighting and tramways services of the city. Captain Cipriani in the course of a debate challenged the Government on the point. The Governor immediately replied. "My opinion was that the City Council was solvent. Whether the statement was made before that the City Council was bankrupt, I have no idea." Obviously the Governor was protecting a subordinate or his immediate predecessor, in other words, the Government, from a damaging admission. Port of Spain is not a remote village; nor a sugar estate. Its estimates come before the Governor every year. The Government could only escape the charge of deliberate misrepresentation by pleading guilty to unpardonable negligence. Captain Cipriani was not speaking on that particular point at the time. But had that been his particular subject, then he as representative of the people of Port of Spain on the Council, as Mayor of the City, and as the man who had seen the malicious despatch in the Colonial Office, might have had severe and justifiable criticisms to make on the action of the Government. But it is certain that as soon as he had begun, the Governor who had made his admission as the head of the Government would have been immediately transformed into His Majesty's representative or the President of the Chamber. And in the Council as it is constituted and with the Governor holding the power that he holds there are never lacking members always on the alert to jump to the defence of the dignity of His Majesty's representative or the respect due to the President of the Chamber, quite neglectful of the responsibility of the head of the administration. There was in that very debate a conspicuous example of this. One nominated member in the course of his address on the Divorce Bill found it necessary to refer to the part the Governor had played in bringing forward that piece of legislation so unpopular with a certain section.

> It is a pity that Your Excellency did not publish these despatches earlier, so that the public might have known the part Your Excellency has played in respect to this matter. I have no doubt that now the despatches have been published and the atmosphere has been clarified, it will be realised that Your Excellency's share of the responsibility for the presentation of this Bill is absolutely nil.
>
> If I may say so without any offence, it would appear that you are regarded by the Colonial Office merely us a servant of the centurion. I say "Come" and he cometh; and I say to another "Go" and he goeth; and I say to my servant "Do this" and he doeth it. It must be very humiliating indeed to any responsible officer to find himself in the position in which Your Excellency must find yourself. It has come to the people of this Colony as a great shock that the administration of this Colony can be treated in the way it has been treated by the Secretary of State.

Now that speech erred, if it erred in any way, on the side of temperance. The speaker was forcible, but his tone was moderate, and certainly it was respectful—in fact, one might have said without exaggeration, so respectful as to be almost humble. But not so in the eyes of one member. No. For him the Governor had been insulted. Nor did he wait for a government official to say so. He began his own address with a flood of compliment to the Solicitor-General for the able way in which he had argued for the Bill, and then turned his hose on to the Attorney-General and complimented him on the able way he had argued against the Bill. Then he switched off to the address of his brother nominated member.

> He referred to the Governor of this Colony in a way ill befitting any member of this Council—certainly a nominated member.

Which gave Captain Cipriani an opportunity to say "Hear, Hear," rejoicing at this open disavowal of the nonsense about nominated members representing the people. But the speaker was not satisfied that enough sacrifices had been offered on the altar of the Governor's dignity. Before his speech was finished he found occasion to make another reference. How the Governor had been treated pained him.

> I was pained to listen to his statement in almost flippant language that the Governor of this Colony was the servant of the centurion; and when the Secretary of State says to come hither, he comes, and when he says to go, he goes!

That was in December, 1931. But a month before, in Dominica, two members of Council, dissatisfied with certain happenings in the Finance Committee, resigned their posts, and gave their reason for doing so. Wrote the Administrator:

> Government House,
> Dominica.
> November 19th, 1931.

> Gentlemen,
>
> The Chairman of the Finance Committee has informed me that you have tendered your resignation on the ground that your endeavours to help in putting the finances of Dominica on a sounder footing are "doomed to be neutralised and defeated," thus reducing your labours "to an absurdity" and infallibly bringing you "into contempt with your constituents."
>
> You then proceed to state that it is His Excellency the Governor who had "stultified" your whole aims and objects, that he has added "insult to injury" by the appointment of one of the Magistrates; and that his "specious plea for economy" does not "impress you as genuine."
>
> 2. Such statements are not only incorrect, but are also most unseemly to use about His Majesty's Representative and are especially improper when coming from members of the Legislative Council; and I should at once accept your resignations were it not that I consider that some further explanation is required from you in the first instance. . . . .

It is not often that this difficulty comes to the surface. But the influence is always present. And it is not only powerful but pernicious. There are, doubtless, good reasons for the head of the Government to sit in the Chair, but on the whole he has no right to be there. In his triple position he exercises a disproportionate influence. His presence is an unfair barrier to free expression of opinion. And a Legislative Council in which a man cannot freely speak his mind, is a place fit for academic debates and not for the discussion of the affairs of government.

I Beg to Congratulate the Government

It is not difficult to imagine the result of all this in the working of the constitution. The Government, overwhelmingly strong as it already is, is without effective criticism or check, and being composed of men who are governing not for the sake of governing, but because they have to make a living, it is not strange that things should be as they are. For the business of government is of such importance to mankind that it must be done under the most vigilant supervision and criticism. There is no need to argue this principle which has proved its value in every modern constitution. "Public life is a situation of power and energy. He trespasses upon his duty who sleeps upon his watch and may as well go over to the enemy." There, Burke, master of political statement, sums up a volume in a phrase. That is the great strength of the English constitution and the two party system. His Majesty's Opposition is an integral part of the British Constitution. Every English minister knows that his work has got to stand the unsparing scrutiny and criticism of a man who very probably occupied the same position just before him and is familiar with the working of the department. This opposition is not necessarily a factious opposition. It is not opposition in the ordinary sense of the word. Rather it is an Opposition. And a Government without a serious Opposition is not the servant of the public but the directors of a limited liability company.

It is the lack of this which robs so much of our politics of any reality. Far from being alert critics, the favourite formula of most of these members is: "I beg to congratulate the Government." Should an official make a speech of no more than mediocre ability, each one, at some time in his own speech, either at the beginning, in the middle or at the end, and sometimes in all three places, "begs to congratulate the honourable member." Always they seem to be bowing obsequiously, hat in hand, always the oily flattery, the ingratiating smile, and criticism offered on a silver salver. A person gaining his first impression of politics from a reading of some of these debates would conclude that it was not the sole business of the Government to govern properly, but a favour that was being conferred upon the people. It must not be imagined that some of these members have been ciphers of no value on the Legislature. Sometimes they are men of great ability and great force of personality. They are men of the world enough to know that if to assert themselves too much is a mistake, it will be equally a mistake to assert themselves too little. They often command a sort of respect, but only up to a point. And they can never have that full weight in public matters which comes from a man like Captain Cipriani, who speaks from his well-known and settled convictions, or from a respected Colonial Secretary, who is stating the case from the Government point of view. Politicians of all kinds and of all countries are notorious self seekers, but as a general rule, whatever their involutions and evolutions, whatever devious routes and pliant ways they may adopt to attain their ends, the majority of them have as the basis of their position, a few settled principles, broad, elastic, strained sometimes almost unbelievably, but nevertheless at least recognisable. Few like Mr. Winston Churchill pass from party to party seeking always whom they may devour. But too often the local unofficial members, whatever their ability, when the crisis really comes are less than nothing. Sometimes they find themselves inadvertently on the wrong side, and it is interesting to see them wriggle out. Can the Government see its way to . . . . ? No. Couldn't the Government . . . . ? No. "I still think I am right, however, though I beg to congratulate the honourable member who explained the Government's position. It is clear that the Government is quite right, too. I beg to congratulate the Government. The Government will hear nothing more of this from me."

It is a serious thing to make such a charge against so important a body of men, but no charges made in this book will be unsubstantiated, and it is necessary to give at once a concrete example of the attitude of these unofficial legislators.

From the time that the Imperial College of Tropical Agriculture started its work in Trinidad there were well-founded complaints of discrimination against coloured men. In April, 1930, there came up before the Legislative Council a grant of eight thousand five hundred pounds a year for five years from the Colonie of Trinidad and Tobago to the Imperial College. Captain Cipriani, as soon as the vote came up, asked the

Government for a definite assurance that there would be no discrimination. Otherwise he would oppose the vote.

Now here for once had arisen above the surface the question which underlies so many matters affecting the people of Trinidad, so many appointments to the higher positions, the rates of pay for certain government servants, the question which underlies the root matter of responsible Government, the question, in fact, which is present at every turn in the affairs of the Colony. Captain Cipriani, having stated his point, sat down. It is very necessary—for this matter finally reached the Colonial Office—to follow the course of the debate which ensued.

> Mr. O'Reilly (who had had a brother there): . . . . I do not follow my honourable friend in suggesting that there has been any discrimination at the College . . . . .
>
> Sir Henry Alcazar: . . . . I do not propose to address you on the question of discrimination. . . . .
>
> The Colonial Secretary read the following statement from the Principal of the Imperial College of Tropical Agriculture:
>
> > I am at a loss to know how the idea has occurred that there is a differentiation over coloured students. So far as the College is concerned there is none. All students are members of the amalgamated clubs. Some coloured men are resident at the Hostel: others reside with relatives or guardians in the neighbourhood, as they find it more convenient and possibly cheaper. But this is the case with all West Indian students, irrespective of colour. All students take luncheon and tea together in any case at the College Hall, and our cricket and other teams are selected by the College Captains, and are comprised of the best men available. There is no trouble, therefore . . . . .
>
> Dr. McShine: Your Excellency, I also supported the desire to have some assurance from the College that the discrimination did not exist or that it was exaggerated, and I am glad to have the explanation, the statement of fact that it is not so . . . . .
>
> Mr. Kelshall: I think that we ought, in looking at this subject, to take a long view. . . . . But I have the utmost confidence in the Head of the College—Mr. Evans—a broad-minded Englishman of the right sort . . . . . and I do not believe there is at present any

ground for complaint in regard to discrimination among the students.

Mr. Wortley (the Director of Agriculture): .... I do feel strongly that the reason is not that the College does not wish them, but that for one reason or another the Trinidadians do not wish to go to the College. In other words, other professions and other openings attract them more.

It remained for the Governor to conclude in the same strain...... We cannot dictate to private companies what appointments they should make, but it appears to me to be very foolish if Companies operating in the country do not appoint people that live here, and prefer to go elsewhere to fill appointments. If I can help in this matter I shall certainly do so. (Applause).

Now here was a debate that from beginning to end was a tissue of lies and hypocrisy. Mr. Gaston Johnston (a coloured man), who was present, did not contribute anything in the House, but when the meeting was over he told Captain Cipriani that Father English, the principal of St. Mary's College, had received a letter from Mr. Martin Leake, the previous Principal of the Agricultural College, in which Mr. Leake had asked Father English to discourage young men of colour from coming to the Imperial College, because although he, the Principal, had nothing against them, the white students made it unpleasant, which caused a great deal of difficulty.

"My God, Johnston, you mean to say that you knew that, and not only did not say so yourself, but did not tell me?"

"No, for if I had told you, you would say it and cause a lot of trouble."

Captain Cipriani was not the man to leave the matter there. He knew, as every other member of Council knew, the true state of affairs at the College. When he went to England in the July following, he made representations to the Colonial Office. The Colonial Office official listened to him, and then took up a copy of Hansard.

"Captain Cipriani, you complain of discrimination. Now, isn't Mr. O'Reilly a coloured man? Yes. Now listen to what he says ..... Isn't Sir Henry Alcazar a coloured man? Now listen to what he says ..... Isn't Mr. Kelshall a coloured man? ..... Isn't Dr. McShine a coloured man?

And this is what he says . . . . . Now, Captain Cipriani, what have you come here making trouble about?"

The dog with the tail between his legs was not in it. Captain Cipriani had to retire. He had not only been made to look like a fool in the eyes of the Colonial Office, but, what was more, would seem to be a man bent on stirring up race feeling for some nefarious purpose of his own.

Now one can understand the position of the white men who spoke in this debate. One can understand Mr. Wortley saying that Trinidadians did not go to the Imperial College because they preferred other avenues, for he stated also that he had not been in the Colony very long. There is less excuse for the Governor, who, after being in the responsible position of head of the Government, could make what was tantamount to a confession that he did not know the Oil Companies would as soon appoint a Zulu chief to some of their higher offices as a local man of colour, whatever the qualifications he had gained at the Imperial College. We can even pass over the statement of Mr. Evans.

"I am at a loss to know how the idea has occurred that there is differentiation over coloured students."

Which is in such direct conflict with the written statement of the previous Principal, Mr. Martin Leake. Englishmen or white men do not wish any discussion of matters of race. They go where they like, do what they like, travel in any part of a ship, are eligible for any position. They stand to gain nothing by talk about race discrimination, and they stand to lose a great deal. But in this debate, as in every other, what is so pitiful is the attitude of these so-called representatives of the people, who so often hold the positions that they do hold because of their colour. The majority of these men hate even more than white men any talk about colour. For if they stand up against colour discrimination they will be noted by the Government and officials as leaders of the people, a real Opposition, and then goodbye to some of their dearest hopes; while for some of them it will mean facing in public the perfectly obvious but nevertheless dreadful fact that they are not white men.

That is the Trinidad Legislature. The reader will now be able to appreciate at its true value statements such as these that the Legislative Council is equally divided between officials, representatives of the Government, and unofficials, representatives of the people, and that the Finance Committee is composed entirely of unofficial members, by which lovers of Crown Colony Government try to make the unwary believe that the control of the money is in the hands of the representatives of the people. It is, so long as these representatives know that they are working within the orbit of the Government's wishes. Sometimes if the Governor anticipates trouble he sends round a confidential circular upon which almost every man Jack spins round and faces in the new direction. There has been one notorious case in which certain members of the Finance Committee rejected a proposal with scorn in the morning, to come back in the afternoon and vote for it.

From this the transition to Captain Cipriani's activities on the Council is easy. It is a case of almost single-handed effort. Now and then a few of the unofficials will give him a lukewarm support. But beyond seconding the motion or delivering a speech carefully calculated not to offend, they do not exert themselves. They will half-kill themselves over measures like the Water Ordinance, in 1903, or Divorce, in 1931, when the white people are split into two sections, one of which they can join. But when it comes to anything affecting the masses of the people, if there is the slightest risk of displeasing the Government these unofficials leave them to their fate without the slightest compunction.

Captain Cipriani's Work

When Captain Cipriani became Mayor of Port of Spain, in his position as Mayor of the city and its representative on the Legislative Council, he started work first on the improvement of the bed of the Dry River, an open sewer which had been poisoning the people living on its banks for generations and a project for the improvement of which had hung fire since 1893. The Government agreed to pay its share and the work is well on the way to completion.

Again, in his double capacity as Mayor and member for Port of Spain, he raised in the House the age-old question of better housing for the poorer classes.

> Meanwhile I have put a question on the point to the Government and what shall I say to the childish, insincere and absurd answer which they have given to my question! It is thrown back to me that the City Council should see after it. Do the advisers of the Government not

know that under the ordinance the City Council has no power? If they do not know that, it is a pity, because it is an ordinance which they themselves have enacted. If the City Council had the power to tackle the housing problem, I assure you they would not come to the Government.

He continued, and backed by the Corporation has been successful. Twelve workers homes have been built and 200 more will soon be built, the Corporation and the Government sharing the expense.

Poor relief, the safety of workers in factories, the health of the people, their proper housing, their education; these are the things which Captain Cipriani is always urging on a lethargic Government.

A Bill to enforce compulsory education was passed in 1921. In 1927, 1928 and 1929 questions were put across this table by myself and answered half-heartedly; we were told that there was no money or that it would be considered or that something would be done next year. On each occasion I failed to draw from the Director of Education what it would cost in pounds, shillings and pence. We are representatives of the taxpayers and if we come and tell the Government that we want compulsory education introduced and are willing to foot the bill, may I ask why is it that the Government refuses to act upon that and introduce compulsory education in Trinidad? The abolition of child labour was introduced here some time ago, and I put it to you it was only as a sop to Cerberus. Cipriani was agitating and so as to stop Cipriani introduce an ordinance for the abolition of child labour! It was introduced but our children are still being pilloried and sweated to-day and the police know it, and can do nothing, because they are helpless and fear to tackle those who are sweating the children. Introduce and enforce the abolition of child labour and compulsory education must follow; but if you allow child labour then you are crippling any effort which we may make in introducing compulsory education in this Colony.

He has done his best to get the Government to institute competitive examinations for entry into the Civil Service but the Government will not let this valuable patronage slip so easily from its hands. Its reply was the usual nonsense about the present system furnishing the Civil Service

..... with men of satisfactory character, and there is no reason to assume that the introduction of the competitive principle of recruitment would produce candidates of higher moral or educational qualities than those who now present themselves from the schools of the Colony.

[Such is] the ancient covering for what in reality amounts to this. We have the power in our hands and we shall hold on to it as long as we can.

Such measures as the Seditious Publications Ordinance and the Habitual Idlers Ordinances are the objects of his constant attack. When will the Government remove them from the Statute Book? Other West Indian islands have removed the Seditious Publications Ordinance, a measure excusable during war time, but an infringement of the liberties of the people in time of peace. The Government in the face of strong opposition from the public passed the Habitual Idlers Ordinance under which they have prosecuted three people. Since 1925 year after year has seen him raising the question in Council, for he resents anything which hints at insult or discrimination against the people who form the bulk of the community.

In 1926 and again in 1929 he asked questions in the House about steamship companies refusing to carry negroes as first class passengers. The Government's reply on one occasion was that the ships which came into the harbour were under no contract with the Government, and therefore, they did not see that it would serve any useful purpose to institute enquiries. Any British Government which gave such a reply to a question in the House of Commons about discrimination being practised in the same way against Englishmen might unloose an agitation which might cost it its place in the end.

Himself the most unassuming of men, he is jealous of his position as representative of the people.

> I do not see why the Hon. Colonial Secretary should try to "tick me off" in the manner he has. I would remind him that I am not at school. I am here representing the people. He on his side has his job to do. I do not object to this. My job is to represent the people and to speak on their behalf, and it is also part of my duty to warn Your Excellency against taking what I consider a false step, and when I make a recommendation to Your Excellency I expect the Government to take it in the spirit of sincerity in which it is meant.

Confidential circulars he does not consider argument.

I still say that the undertaking was given to the Finance Committee, not for the Garrison Quartermaster, but for the Staff Officers; and when I say that the opinions of the members of the Finance Committee changed, and changed as the result of Your Excellency's confidential circular, I am not disputing your right to issue them. I am only stressing the fact that it did have this effect on the Finance Committee and it has had that effect on two occasions of late. One was the question of the appointment of an Assistant Director of Agriculture and to-day the Staff Officer. The Finance Committee voted solidly that there would be no appointment of Assistant Director of Agriculture, they voted solidly that there would be no appointment of Staff Officer, but immediately on Your Excellency's Minute being issued to them they have changed their opinions. Rightly or wrongly, that is a matter of fact. I have no criticism to offer to Your Excellency on those Confidential Circulars. The only position I take up is this, that I cannot interpret them as being a direction from Your Excellency as to how I should vote: that I should vote according to Your Excellency's recommendations in them. . . . .

It would be a mistake to think, however, that he takes a narrow view of what concerns the welfare and interests of the people. A mere cursory examination of the pages of Hansard would show that no one is more interested in the development of the sugar industry, the cocoa industry, and agriculture generally, which it is his firm belief is the ultimate basis of the economic life of the community. He has even published a pamphlet on the sugar question.

At present, owing to the constitution, he is an influence more than a force. Two episodes will show as well as anything else, the first, the weight of inertia, and the second, the unscrupulousness with which he has to contend. In 1929 he asked the Government if it would take the necessary steps to institute a system of Old Age Pensions in the Colony. Few of the social services have given so little dissatisfaction to even the sternest opponents of the oncoming march of the working classes. But it is curious how the members of the local Government are not ashamed to confess absolute ignorance on matters which are common knowledge among educated persons far less among others whose business it is to keep themselves in touch with all such questions. The Government's reply to Captain Cipriani was this:

> Before a definite reply can be given to the question of the Honourable Member, it will clearly be necessary to collect full data as to the actual position in the Colony and to ascertain the results of experience in other places where the principle has been applied. The Government has no objection to undertaking these preliminaries, and will take steps to institute such enquiries.

Let us admit in all good faith that the Government has to be cautious with a measure entailing permanent expenditure. Every reasonable person will be whole-heartedly with the Government up to that point. But watch that answer a little more closely. The Government does not care two straws about Old Age Pensions really. "The Government has no objection." Inasmuch as the Hon. Member asked, the Government has no objection. But it is not too much to read into the answer that if the Hon. Member did not ask, no such thing would ever cross the mind of the Government. And, as a fact, up to the time of writing, no more has been heard of it, neither will any more be heard unless Captain Cipriani raises the question again and again and yet again. But it is amazing to note the courage and persistence he brings to this disheartening work, meeting after meeting. The taxation of the oil industry, the second example, is a case in point. The people of Trinidad have long felt that the oil industry was not paying its fair share of taxation in the Colony.

In 1922 the Under-Secretary of State, interviewed on the oil question, said that the question of an export tax was "clearly one for the local government." There the matter stayed until the Legislative Council in 1925 received Captain Cipriani among the elected members. In 1926, he asked the Government a question. The Government replied that it had no intention of imposing any tax. In 1926 Captain Cipriani made a formal motion. The oil industry was flourishing, it employed the least labour, it might come to an end at any minute. In five years the Apex Company had paid £340,000, or 85 per cent. of the capital, and had the remaining 15 per cent. in hand nearly twice over.

The motion was carried without a dissentient voice: the case was too glaring.

In 1927 Captain Cipriani asked if anything had been done. The Government said that certain proposals had been found impracticable, but the question had not been lost sight of, and would be made the subject of a special enquiry in the near future. Twice again in 1929, once in May and once again in November, Captain Cipriani questioned the Government, asking in November whether the steps for deriving greater revenue laid down in the Report on the oil industry by Sir Thomas Holland would be carried out. The Government said that it was in communication with the Secretary of State. He tried again in May, 1930. But up to to-day, 1932, despite that motion passed without a dissentient voice in 1926, nothing has been done. The Chamber of Commerce is the local Government, and the local Government is the Chamber of Commerce.

That is the Legislative Council of a Crown Colony Government, generally speaking. We need not go an inch out of Captain Cipriani's life to see it on every conceivable occasion doing its damnedest. Two important questions remain which we will allow to speak for themselves. First, then, for the matter of the electric lights and tramway services of the City of Port of Spain, and then afterwards for the Divorce Bill. The first is a tale primarily of bad faith and to a lesser degree of blundering, the second primarily of blundering and to a lesser degree of bad faith.

CHAPTER VI

The Municipality and
the Trinidad Electric Company

It was Alderman Richards (founder of the Workingmen's Association) who, some time in 1928, asked two questions at a City Council meeting.

> Was His Worship the Mayor aware that the franchise granted to the Trinidad Electric Company Ltd. would expire in the near future?
> If the answer is in the affirmative, would His Worship consider the advisability of Municipal ownership of all tramways and electric services within the City?

Later, Alderman Richards drew the attention of the Mayor to the fact that the Electric Light and Tramway Company of Jamaica paid to the Jamaica Government in taxation annually the sum of £5,000 and to the Jamaica City Corporation an additional 4 per cent. of the gross revenue, while in Trinidad the Electric Light and Power Company, a private company, was paying nothing at all for the concession which it had been enjoying for the past 28 years, neither to the Government nor to the Municipality.

The City Council's first move was to ask Mr. C. A. Child, K.C., Barrister-at-Law, for an opinion on the ordinances under which the Company held the contract. In December, 1929, the City Council received Mr. Child's opinion. He wrote that it was for the Governor-in-Executive-Council to decide in the first instance whether an extension of the franchise was to be granted to the Trinidad Electric Company Ltd., and if he decided that such an extension was to be granted, the City Council would have no right to acquire the undertaking. But should the Governor-in-Council decide not to extend the franchise, then the Governor and the City Council each had the right to purchase the undertaking. In such event, as Mr. Child saw it, the one which first gave notice to the Trinidad Electric Company requiring them to sell their undertaking would be the party entitled to acquire.

The next step was to approach the Government which at the City Council's request promised to send for an expert to conduct an independent investigation. The City Council agreed to pay his expenses. The Government then appointed a Committee to consider the matter. This Committee consisted of the Director of Public Works; the Government Wireless Engineer; the Mayor, Captain Cipriani; Alderman Gaston Johnston, K.C. (who had been five times Mayor of the City), under the chairmanship of the Attorney-General. The Committee sent in a unanimous report on the 11th April. The Committee was of opinion that:

> the evidence before the Committee indicated that the purchase of the Electric Lighting and Tramways undertaking and their running as a going concern would be a sound business proposition, and should, if properly controlled, lead to a cheaper service.

In regard to the question of future ownership, the Committee stated that it did not recommend the Government to purchase the undertaking unless

> (a) The Port-of-Spain City Council is unwilling to take over the undertaking, and
>
> (b) The Electric Company is not prepared to submit to substantial modifications in the existing concession, and in particular, with regard to the maximum prices for energy supplied (vide fourth schedule to Cap. 310), which, in our opinion, should be a condition precedent to the consideration of any extension of the franchise. The consideration of "b" will not arise, we think, if the Municipality is desirous of purchasing.

So far all was plain sailing, and the thing seemed settled when Mr. Parry, the expert, reported as follows:—

> The alternative to a non-renewal of the Franchise is purchase either by the Government or by the Municipality of Port-of-Spain. According to the interpretations of sections 120 and 121, the first option rests with the Government, but as far as I can gather there does not seem to be any great desire on the part of the Government to acquire the undertaking while the Municipal Authorities are very keen

to take control. Of the two parties the Municipal Authorities are more directly interested in the management of the undertaking, more particularly because the tramways form an integral part of the works covered by the ordinance, and it is highly desirable to say the least, that all matters affecting the street traffic and the construction of permanent way, etc., should be in the hands of the Municipal Authorities.

But one disquieting aspect of the matter from the City Council point of view was that Mr. Parry whom they had asked the Government to send for and whose expenses and fees they were paying was handled not by them but entirely by the Government, and his report was sent to the Government who only by courtesy allowed the Council to see a copy. Meanwhile, Mr. F. B. McCurdy, President of the Trinidad Electric Company accompanied by Counsel came to Trinidad early in 1930. This was Mr. McCurdy's second visit in recent times. He had come to Trinidad in the December before and he and Mr. De Nobriga, Manager of the Company, had been entertained noticeably often at Government House by Mr. Grier, then Acting Governor, a very indiscreet thing for Mr. Grier to do. Trouble was certainly ahead in regard to this question. As Colonial Secretary, he would have to play an important part in the negotiations. Any careful administrator, though he may have found it necessary to feed the President of the Canadian Company, would have at least taken care to feed him with a very long spoon.

These representatives of the Canadian Company made certain proposals to the Government. These were: that the earnings of the Company should be limited to 10 per cent. of the value of its property after providing a reasonable amount for depreciation and a contingent reserve, and secondly, that in lieu of all the taxes the Company should pay to the Government a sum equal to 2 per cent of its gross revenue from the electric service and tramway service, part of which might be paid by the Government to the City of Port-of-Spain as compensation for the use of the streets. These terms were finally embodied in a letter to the Colonial Secretary who communicated them to the City Council and invited the City Council to meet the Governor.

> His Excellency: Gentlemen, I have invited you to meet to-day to consider the question of the Trinidad Electric Company's franchise which, as you are aware, terminates in March next.

Captain Cipriani: We have decided to take over the Trinidad Electric Company, and we do not feel that we should be called upon to consider any proposals from the Trinidad Electric Company. We interpret the ordinance to mean that in the event of the Government not wishing to take over the Company the City Council come forward and say "We take over," and we do not consider that the City Council is under any obligation to listen to proposals from the present Company.

His Excellency: Would it not be wiser to hear those proposals before definitely making up your minds?

Captain Cipriani: No, because I do not see what proposals they could possibly have. If they put up better proposals than exist at the present it only means that we should be tied down to a private company for another short period, at the end of which time the difficulties are going to be the same as they are to-day.

Mr. Maillard: I do not see why we should not listen to any proposals without prejudice.

His Excellency: Their charges are at present, in my opinion, high, but perhaps they may propose to make them less.

Captain Cipriani: The other point is that the Government is in sympathy with the Company if they wish to carry on. It seems so.

His Excellency: I do not see how you can know whether we are in sympathy with the Company if they wish to carry on.

Captain Cipriani: The gestures of the Government so far, lead us to suppose that. I question the right of the Government to try to induce us to adopt that attitude and accept new proposals from the Company. We have had them operating for the last 25 or 30 years, and we have had nothing from them. Until you say that the Colonial Office say we are to accept the proposals, speaking for myself, if a meeting is convened for us to listen to the T.E.C. I will not attend and I will advise the members of the City Council not to attend. The Government can explore the ground, and they can listen to what the Company has to say, but we are not going to be a party to any three-party meeting.

His Excellency: I am sorry to hear you speak like that. It sounds as though you are prejudiced.

Captain Cipriani: I am prejudiced.

His Excellency: I think it only fair and right that we should hear what the Company has to say. If you refuse to hear them I cannot coerce you, but I think it would be a pity. We, as a Government, must explore the ground and hear what their proposals are.

Whatever were the inferences which Captain Cipriani drew from the attitude of the Government, there could be no mistaking the tone of the final paragraph of a letter from the Colonial Secretary, Mr. Grier, to the Town Clerk.

I am to add that the Government is not prepared to give financial assistance to or to guarantee a loan for the purpose of acquiring the undertaking at present controlled by the Company until a full investigation has shown that such acquisition would be in the public interest.

(Signed) S. M. GRIER,
Colonial Secretary.

Now here was an attitude provocative and vexatious to the last degree. In accordance with practice all over England, a practice to-day accepted not only in theory but in fact, the City Council, duly elected representatives of the people of Port of Spain, had unanimously decided that they wished to acquire the rights of the Company for themselves, in as much as the Government did not want them. As the Under-Secretary of State for the Colonies informed the City Council delegation when, as was finally found necessary, they put the matter before him, municipal ownership of power and tramways had been the accepted policy in Great Britain for many years, and the result of the policy had been of the greatest benefit to the ratepayers of the municipalities. The City Council had done all in their power to do and had done it in a way with which no fault could be found. They had had legal advice, they had submitted the matter to the Government, the Government had itself appointed a Committee, which had reported unanimously in favour of the City Council taking over, and the soundness of the undertaking as a business proposition. The City Council had requested and agreed to pay the expenses of an expert from England invited here for the sole purpose of investigating the question of the City Council's taking over. His report had been wholly favourable. Yet, after two years, and when matters seemed settled, the Council now had to face a new attitude on the part of the Government, with the final absurdity of a letter from the Colonial Secretary talking about the necessity of a full investigation.

But Captain Cipriani was equal to the position. He wrote a Minute to the City Council.

> ..... The Government in its eagerness to press for a decision favourable to the Trinidad Electric Company during the ensuing eight days, opens itself to the severest possible criticism, and I regret to have to describe its haste as indecent, immoral and in direct contravention to the provisions of the ordinance, as interpreted by this Council, and supported by the opinion of the legal gentleman in London to whom the matter was referred by the Government and a copy of whose opinion is also laid before you.
>
> In the above circumstances, it is my duty, as Mayor of this City, to prepare you for a grim, deliberate and determined constitutional fight, in the best interests of the Municipality, as the sacred principles of democratic institutions are being mercilessly assailed, and that, too, without foundation or reason.
>
> In my opinion, the time has come for this Council to put its house in order, and to take the necessary safeguards for obtaining the best legal, as well as technical, advice as can be procured with a view to making the strongest possible representation to the Colonial Office.
>
> In this constitutional struggle, I feel confident of the whole-hearted support of the citizens of Port of Spain, and of the entire Colony's inhabitants, and rely upon this Council for its loyal and united support in what is only another struggle for the cause of right against might.
>
> ARTHUR A. CIPRIANI.

On the 11th June, the representatives of the City Council again met His Excellency the Governor, Sir Claud Hollis, who read a statement. Sir Claud Hollis, neglecting the evidence of the Government Committee and of Mr. Parry, based his arguments on a valuation of the property made by Mr. Harding in 1927. This valuation, the Company's Directors had told him, put the property at one million eight hundred thousand dollars. The cost of [an] additional generating plant would be one hundred and forty thousand dollars, and this information also Sir Claud had received from the Company. The total cost to the City Council would, therefore, be two million four hundred and forty thousand dollars. The cost of arbitration proceedings would be considerable, and in as much as Mr. Parry had stated that the capital value of the undertaking as a going concern to the Government or the Municipality was one million five hundred thousand dollars, His Excellency had therefore . . . .

In conclusion I feel that I must say a few words regarding the action which His Worship the Mayor saw fit to take by communicating to the Press his Minute of May 29th. The wording of this Minute is intemperate in expression, and I regard it as regrettable that he should have issued what amounts to a call on the people of this Colony to oppose the Government.

From the Government point of view, the whole question resolves itself into whether an adequate and efficient supply of electric light and power can be secured at cheaper rates by the acquisition of the undertaking by the Government or by the Municipality than by the grant of a different type of franchise to the Company.

Captain Cipriani replied:

It seems to me that there is nothing for me to answer except the criticisms which you have levelled at me in what you have just read, and reluctantly to express my opinion that there seems no good reason why I should retract or withdraw one single word in my statement to the Council or in public.

The Government from the very outset made it plain that their intention was to explore the ground, and that if the Company put to them a reasonable proposal for the extension of a new franchise they would be inclined to receive such a proposal sympathetically. That proposal was in direct opposition with the wishes of the people of this Colony and of the Municipality, and therefore, as Mayor of this City, I feel it is my duty to take the stand I have. . . . . . and therefore I cannot be a party to casting this slur on the City Council now, by telling us in so many words that "you are not a body fit to be entrusted with the electric light and tramway undertaking." A shopkeeper in any part of the Colony could run the undertaking, and for the Government to build anything on what Mr. Harding has said is no concern of mine. Harding was a reliable and honest man the while he was employed by the Company, but the moment he leaves them becomes dishonest and not to be trusted. But I still hope that the position of the Government is that they are behind the Municipality and not behind the Canadian Company.

Every man has his own conception of what his duty is, and I am going to play my part honestly and fearlessly as long as I have the power and energy to put it before the people. This is my country. I was born and bred in it. I have lived all my life here, and I am certainly not going to be deprived of anything to which I consider I have the privilege, by the local or any other Government, without making a clear, honest and truthful fight for it.

Mr. Gaston Johnston then explained that there was no detailed inventory on which the Company could base its claim to value the property at one million eight hundred thousand dollars. At one time there was some reorganisation and shuffling of the Company in Canada which resulted in Mr. McCurdy acquiring the major portion of the shares. That valuation appeared over Mr. Harding's signature because he was forced to sign it.

By this time the Council was thoroughly alarmed, and decided to send a delegation to the Colonial Office. Speed was imperative, and the Council brushed aside the legal technicalities which might have impeded action. Everywhere in England, the delegation was most sympathetically received. Mr. Morrison, the Minister of Transport, granted them an interview. He said his experience was that Municipalities managed their electrical undertakings with great success and with resulting benefit to the taxpayers. He instanced his own district, Woolwich, where he paid for electric power the sum of three farthings per unit. But in fact everybody knows that except a Crown Colony Government. Mr. Morrison promised that his own department would help Port of Spain in every way when the undertaking was taken over. But the most extraordinary experience of the delegation was to learn that the local Government in its despatches to the Secretary of State had drawn the attention of the Colonial Office to the fact that for the year 1930 the Municipality had financed for an estimated expenditure which was greatly in excess of its estimated revenue. A statement of that kind made without giving at the same time an explanation of the policy of the Municipality in preparing the estimates, was apt to create the impression that the City Council was reckless in its methods of finance, and therefore, as a natural corollary, unfit for handling such a big undertaking as taking over the lighting and transport services. That, at any rate, was the impression made on the Colonial Office. Luckily the delegation was well armed with all the necessary documents, and had no difficulty in convincing the Colonial Office of the soundness both of the Municipality's methods of financing and its financial position. The Mayor and the Town Clerk had the satisfaction of hearing that their methods were those used by many of the best-run municipalities in England. The Government's complaint to the Colonial Office is all the more inexplicable when it is remembered that, as is required by law, the municipal estimates for 1930 had been approved by the Governor and Legislative Council without criticism or comment. But it must be stated in fairness to the Government that while the deputation was in England, it saw at the Colonial Office a later letter, the contents of which were calculated to remove any unfortunate impression which the previous despatch had created.

The going of the delegation gave the opportunity to those who make it their business to oppose and to run down anything which is done by local people to speak of the waste of public money and the uselessness of the venture. But sometime after its return, however (the Electric Company had meanwhile taken the matter to the Courts), the Town Clerk received a letter from Mr. Nankivell, the Acting Colonial Secretary.

> I am directed to inform you that a despatch has been addressed to the Secretary of State for the Colonies, informing him that in the event of the Trinidad Electric Company losing their appeal to the Privy Council, the Governor intends to refuse any application which the Company may make to extend the existing franchise and to give the Municipality the opportunity of acquiring the undertaking.

So that at the time of writing everything depends on the decision of the Privy Council, and should the Company lose its appeal the City Council will have the right of taking over.

It will be worth while to turn over and read the final paragraph of Mr. Grier's letter and compare it with Mr. Nankivell's. Between the two letters there has been no further investigation, no further enquiry, absolutely nothing except the trip of the delegation. No. There was something else.

Feeling that some explanation was due to account for all its doubling and twisting, the Government said that it had had in mind a comprehensive scheme of lighting the city and the outlying districts. But that fell flat. Nobody bothered with it, and the Government's last spurt was to carry on a heated correspondence with the Town Clerk about the expenses of the delegation. Much ink was spilt as to whether the delegation should have paid for its own deck chairs or not.

During the struggle over the franchise of the Electric Company, Captain Cipriani twice found himself in contact with the Government, apart from his duties as Mayor and legislator.

He had stood surety to the extent of £200 for the Editor of the "Labour Leader," which at one time was the organ of the Working Men's Association. The "Labour Leader" libelled an Inspector of Constabulary, who was awarded damages and costs amounting to nearly £500. It was the duty of the Government to collect this money, and on the 8th April, 1930, Captain Cipriani received a letter from the Crown Solicitor and Administrator General.

> . . . . . I am further instructed to notify you that unless the sum of £200 be paid me on or before the 15th inst., proceedings will be commenced against you on the Bond without further notice.
>
> Captain Cipriani replied asking for three months time:
>
> I do not think you will expect me to find such a large sum as £200 within so short a time as seven days in these times.

The Crown Solicitor replied that he would be given ten days.
Captain Cipriani then wrote to the Governor direct:

> No explanation was vouchsafed to me as to why "my request could not be complied with," leaving it to be inferred, either that compliance was refused by the Government on personal grounds, or that some public financial catastrophe would occur if the Government did not get the money within the mentioned period of seven or ten days. I feel that neither of these suggestions is correct. . . . . .

Captain Cipriani pointed out that the principal, the actual defendant, had not been first proceeded against, which was the normal course. Secondly, persons convicted of criminal offences were usually given time to pay. He failed to see why he should be hounded down in this manner.

The Governor granted an extension of time.

Captain Cipriani is far from being a rich man. A public subscription was started in the "Port of Spain Gazette," and the money simply rolled in. Groups of working men from all parts of the country sent in their shillings and sixpences, and in a short time the money was paid.

A few weeks after, just before Captain Cipriani left Trinidad for the Labour Conference in England during the summer of 1930, he had an interview with Sir Claud Hollis. In the course of it the Governor told Captain Cipriani he thought the Captain was the person most suitable to take up the position of Inspector of Poor Relief under the provisions on an ordinance then contemplated. His Excellency stated that he had arrived at that conclusion by reason of the great interest Captain Cipriani took in the section of the community most likely to benefit under the new Poor Relief Laws. Sir Claud made it very clear that the decision of the Government was not to be taken as a measure to "buy him off," or words to that effect.

Captain Cipriani replied that he would be pleased to accept the appointment provided that it did not interfere with his political activities, and he certainly did not consider the offer a ruse. The Governor said he did not think Captain Cipriani's acceptance of the post would interfere, and said he was pleased at his willingness to consider the proposal favourably.

The Governor stated that the salary attached to the post would be about £700 a year, and £200 a year travelling allowance.

When Captain Cipriani returned from England he called on the Governor, who again introduced the subject of the appointment, but now stated that his advisors said the office would have to be held by a whole time officer. Captain Cipriani said it was with great regret he, therefore, refused the other. The regret was due to the fact that he considered the administration of Poor Relief very important work which could only be properly carried out by persons who knew local conditions and who were interested in the people. There the matter dropped.

Somehow news of the offer got into the newspapers, where the amount offered as salary was mentioned, with the usual newspaper exaggeration, as £1,200 a year. Naturally, people began to laugh, and the Government did not cut a very heroic figure in the comments that were passed. The Government did not like what was being said, and Mr. Grier, the Colonial Secretary, wrote a letter to Captain Cipriani, a letter which was as creditable to his powers of diplomacy as it was unconvincing to the public. Certain paragraphs must be reproduced in full:

> I am to remind you that at an interview which you had with the Governor before proceeding to England, His Excellency asked whether in the event of such an appointment being approved you desired to be considered for the post, and was given to understand that you did so wish it provided that the duties of the post did not interfere with your political work.
>
> It was subsequently decided to make the appointment a whole time one, and His Excellency therefore told you when you came to see him a few days ago that there could be in consequence no question of offering it to you.
>
> The pay of the post has been fixed by the Estimates Committee at £300 per annum, plus £200 travelling allowance. There was never any intention of the post carrying a salary of £1,200 and travelling allowance.
>
> I am to inform you that copies of this letter are being communicated to the Press.
>
> I have the honour to be, Sir,
> Your obedient servant,
> S. M. GRIER,
> Colonial Secretary.

Admirable as Mr. Grier's letter was in both suppression and suggestion, it could have no effect. The Government, with singular obtuseness, did not understand Captain Cipriani well enough to know that it would require another sort of lime to snare that bird; it did not know the public well enough to know that it would never believe Captain Cipriani guilty of hanging round any Governor for a job—least of all a job of £300 a year.

Captain Cipriani sent the papers on to the Secretary of State for the Colonies, since when nothing more has been heard of this discreditable episode.

Even while the Government was ruining its prestige over the Tramways and Power question, it was entangling itself slowly but inextricably in the toils of the Divorce Legislation. The surface details of this are so few and so well-known that barely the shortest reference to them is needed. In 1926, Mr. O'Reilly proposed the introduction of Divorce Legislation into the Colony. The Governor used the official vote to throw the motion out. The Catholic element in the community was very strong. The leaders of the Protestants were against it. The large majority of the Protestants were mildly interested. The masses of the people were on the whole quite indifferent or rather amused. The Governor said that there was no demand, and it would be unwise to force through such a measure. Unfortunately, the Colonial Office took a different view, and pestered the local Government. Between the Colonial Office and the steadily increasing agitation of the Anti-Divorcists, the Government lost its head completely. It showed itself unable to deal either with its slaves at home or its masters abroad. It is more than probable that the Colonial Office regrets its attitude in this matter and the consequences which have followed. Had the local Government transmitted a clear idea of the political situation in the West Indies to the Colonial Office at home, it is difficult to believe that the Colonial Office would have forced the point as it did, for from one point of view the whole Divorce adventure was on the part of the Government nothing more nor less than a piece of colossal stupidity. In Trinidad (broadly speaking) there are the whites and the blacks. The blacks, particularly the working people, were admitted to be growing daily more politically conscious and clamouring for Trade Unions and self-government and all sorts of uncomfortable things which are as gall in the mouth of a Crown Colony Government. The white people, at one in their desire to keep the blacks in their places, are themselves divided into two classes, the English official and industrial group, mainly.Protestant, and the white creole, mainly Roman Catholic. With the blacks already restive and the political weather cloudy, where was the sense from the government point of view in antagonising the leaders of one of the remaining sections by going through with the Divorce Bill, particularly when the leader of the masses and the leader of the Catholics was one and the same person?

We shall follow this Divorce question closely. For here we have the opportunity to see how men behave when given a free hand over people whom they have been trained to regard as inferior, whose inferiority indeed is implicit in the form of government. The writer will intrude for a moment to say that he is neither Catholic nor anti-Divorce. His personal views, however, leave the facts unchanged.

I want the reader to step back for a moment with me to the greatest catastrophe which has ever befallen Trinidad since it is under British rule. I refer to the riot of 1908. The riot owed its origin to the wish of the Government to introduce a perfectly good piece of legislation dealing with the water supply. The Government introduced it in such a way that there was rioting, the Government buildings were burnt down, fourteen people were killed and over forty wounded, the Governor and the Colonial Secretary left the service, and to this day the Bill is not on the Statute Book. This was the note-worthy occasion when just before the Legislative Council meeting began the excited crowd was stimulated to action by the sight of the Hon. the Director of Public Works and the Hon. the Colonial Secretary standing in the corridor, singing "God save the King," and jeering at the crowd below. The Commissioners sent out by the British Government afterwards stated among many other things that there was a large and regrettable division of opinion between the Government and an influential section of the people. One need only read the cross-examination of the then Colonial Secretary, Sir Courtenay Knollys, to recognise why this was so. Yet, whoever compares the two agitations will see that the later Government had learnt nothing from the earlier.

The preliminary situation was just the same, acute dissatisfaction with the form of government and those administering it.

Mr. (afterwards Sir) Henry Alcazar to the Commisioners.

May, 1903.

With the great spread of education a large number of people are now competent to take a great interest in public affairs, and it is quite clear that the time has come when we must be governed differently to the way we are now governed. If any attempt is made to govern this Colony as the hordes of Africa are governed, at the point of the bayonet, the result can only be disastrous. We have not got centuries of civilisation at our back, but we have three-fourths of a century, and much can be accomplished and much has been accomplished in that time. . . . .

Captain Cipriani in the Legislature.

November, 1930.

Before the Labour Commonwealth Conference in 1928 we made the same claim that we again brought forward in 1930, namely, that the people of this Colony have got the education, the ability, the civilisation, and the necessary culture to administer their own affairs.

Crown Colony rule might have been ideal 50 or 100 years ago. Crown Colony rule may still be ideal for the primitive races and for peoples just emerged from slavery. Crown Colony rule may be well for the jungle and the wilds of Africa, but it has outlived its usefulness in these Colonies. . . . .

There was the same dissatisfaction in 1903 as in 1930–1931 with the spending of the people's money, a dissatisfaction which had penetrated in 1903 even to some of those who would ordinarily be staunch supporters of the Government.

Proceedings of Riot Commission.

Mr. Alcazar: Do you consider that the Finance Committee has no power, and therefore it is useless to attend? Have you not on several occasions so expressed yourself?

Mr. Townsend Fenwick (a sugar magnate): I have.

Mr. Alcazar: And in all probability if there was a meeting of the Finance Committee called you did not attend.

Mr. Townsend Fenwick: No, I have always attended whenever summoned, unless I have been prevented by some unavoidable cause.

Mr. Alcazar: Although you consider their proceedings were entirely useless.

Mr. Townsend Fenwick: Well, I have criticised them very strongly at times; but still I have thought it is my duty to attend them.

Captain Cipriani in the Legislature.

.... It might be just as well if no Finance Committee sat at all! If that is the feeling with which the Government is going to accept recommendations from the Finance Committee, then I suppose the sooner we shut down the Finance Committee and let the Government run it the better for all concerned. I won't waste my time to come here and be made a puppet of! When I give my advice I expect it to be given full weight in the same way as I expect the advice of the Government to be given the full weight to which it is entitled. But I refuse to have recommendations of the Finance Committee turned down as this was turned down with not a word of any sentiment or sympathy, but just to tell us that it has been turned down!

There was the same dissatisfaction with the Government's persistent neglect of the masses of the people—always a thing for governments to watch in a small community when voiced by popular and able men. This gets home to the people as nothing else can.

Mr. Alcazar to the Commissioners.

1903.

I have said that I challenge an examination of the Statute Book of this Colony to see whether during the last ten or fifteen years there have been any measures carried by the Government, for those purposes which are surely the primary object of every Government— the alleviation of the labouring classes and the masses of the people, the improvement of sanitation and like matters. Let us take a few examples. We have on the Statute Book of the Colony a Health Ordinance which is about fifty years behind the age, and similarly with regard to the Building Ordinance. Although attempts have been made from time to time to bring these Ordinances up-to-date, they have not been successful. You have heard Mr. Wrightson state in the box that the barrack-yards and the houses of the poor in this city are in an abominably insanitary condition. Then I ask whose fault is that. The Health Ordinance of this Colony is forty years old. No attempt has been made to amend that Ordinance and get powers to remedy this insanitary condition of the place. Surely the Government could have introduced an Ordinance amending the old Ordinance if they had chosen, and could have carried it through irrespective of opposition; possibly there would have been a certain amount of opposition from some of the unofficial members, but the Government, with their majority, could have carried through any measure of this sort. But no, they are content to go on under a Health Ordinance which is forty years old.

Captain Cipriani in the Legislature.

1929.

The Government know—it is no secret—the terrible toll taken of the labouring classes by tuberculosis and ankylostomiasis in this Colony. The Government also know what are the remedial and preventive measures, but what have they done besides making their usual empty promises in the past, as they are willing to make in the future, and will make again this morning. The time was not very long ago—when Sir Samuel Wilson was Governor. . . . .

I happened to discuss with him the necessity of erecting a sanatorium, and reminded him of the promise made by Sir John Chancellor that there would be no golf course on the St. James' pasture until the sanatorium was erected. There has been no meeting of the Tuberculosis Association called since. The golf course exists, but the Sanatorium has not yet been started and possibly never will, unless we, the people of this Colony, bring sufficient pressure on the Government to make them realise what their responsibility is, not only to the classes, but to the masses of the labouring people of this Colony. . . . . The percentage of ankylostomiasis in Couva is 98 per cent., and possibly 100 per cent. The Government has done nothing, and why? Because it would mean bringing pressure to bear on the factory owners to put up modern and progressive latrine accommodation on the estates, and to enable the labouring classes to live in houses fit for human habitation and not fit for the habitation of pigs. That is the only reason why the Government have failed to do their duty.

There was also the danger, pointed out before, of making the influential Catholics anti-Government. In fact, Sir Claud Hollis, the Governor, saw that. But the Colonial Office kept on asking questions about the Divorce Bill, and the Government had to go through, if not introducing at least accepting it when a private member brought it in. Here, then, was a situation calling for delicate and skilful handling. Instead, the Government proceeded on the identical lines which had led to the disaster of 1903.

When we compare the actual course of events in 1903 and in 1930–1931 the parallelism is far more exact.

The Government showed the same inability to answer simple questions in a simple way, the same habit of trying to treat responsible people like children, the same downright rudeness. Note the persistent evasion of Mr. Leotaud's question with the shallow impertinence at the end.

Question in the Legislature on the Water Supply.

1902.

Mr. Leotaud said.... From what he had heard outside there seemed to be a growing feeling that the water works at Diego Martin and St. Clair were not likely to yield the quantity of water the Director of Public Works had estimated....

The Colonial Secretary replied: I am directed to inform the Honourable Member that the works at Diego Martin are not sufficiently advanced to afford an increase to the existing water supply of the town....

Mr. Leotaud said he would have liked the Director of Public Works to have made a few remarks on the subject.

The Director of Public Works replied that he was afraid he could not give any definite answer. He fancied it depended chiefly on the Council voting additional funds.

The Hon. C. Leotaud said his friend Mr. Marryat and himself would like to know whether the Government had a sufficient sum in hand to carry out the scheme for providing Port of Spain with an adequate water supply....

His Excellency said this question hardly arose on the Estimates, as the funds for the purpose came out of loan moneys.

Mr. Leotaud said the answers of the Director of Public Works to previous questions had left a doubt on the minds of members on his side of the table....

The President said the Director of Public Works might be in a better position to give the hon. member an answer.

The Director of Public Works said he could Answer in a very short way; **but perhaps his answer would be too short for the hon. member to understand** . . . .

Mr. Leotaud: Then shall we have a full supply in 1903?

The Director of Public Works said yes, **if no unforeseen fires deforested the Diego Martin valleys and the fall of rain from the skies remained as usual** . . . .

Questions by "Port of Spain Gazette."
4th November, 1930.

(a) Whether there is any truth in the statement that instructions have been received by the local Government, from the Secretary of State, on the subject of Divorce.

(b) Whether, in the event of a Resolution for introduction of Divorce in the Colony being brought before the Legislature by one of the Unofficial Members, it is the intention of the Government to allow free voting on same, that is to say, allow the officials to vote as they please.

ANSWER:

The Colonial Secretary regretted his inability to reply.

Questions by "Port of Spain Gazette."
1st December, 1930.

(3) In view of the fact that it is persistently rumoured that a Bill intended to give to the Supreme Court of this Colony jurisdiction to decree the dissolution of Christian Marriages will shortly be introduced into the Legislative Council, we would be pleased to know if:

(a) The Government of this Colony has any instruction to introduce such a Bill.

(b) If the Government of this Colony has been asked by the Colonial Office to ascertain the wishes of the community in relation to Divorce.

(c) If the Government of the Colony has any knowledge of the intention of any member of the Legislative Council to obtain leave to introduce such a Bill.

ANSWER:

The Colonial Secretary must point out to the Editor of the "Port of Spain Gazette" that answers to questions, whether communications on this or any other subject have or have not passed between this Government and the Secretary of State, will not be given from this office. **The Colonial Secretary knows of no justification for the persistent rumours to which the Editor refers.**

Anyone would have seen that the "Gazette" had information and was trying to force the Government's band.

The Colonial Secretary was quite within his rights to refuse to answer, but, knowing the peremptory dispatches which the Secretary of State had already written, and aware, as he must have been aware, that the "Gazette" was getting ready to fight to the last ditch, it was a grave and unnecessary blunder to go on to say that he knew of no justification . . . . . a blunder of which when the time came the newspaper made extensive use.

To continue. The Government showed in 1903, as in 1931, the same unbusinesslike habits amounting to contempt in its method of correspondence with the leaders of the opposition.

Proceedings of Riot Commission.

1903.

Mr. Alcazar: I take it you took the trouble to ascertain whether the Government is in possession of any such correspondence.

The Colonial Secretary: I had not the opportunity of ascertaining.

Mr. Alcazar: You had not?

The Colonial Secretary: No.

Mr. Alcazar: The Solicitor wrote to you an official letter asking for that correspondence. Surely your duty was to enquire whether there was any such correspondence or not before writing to him and telling him that the Government is not in possession of any such correspondence.

Later:—

Mr. Alcazar: . . . . did you, before sending that reply, enquire from the Director of the Public Works Department or from any official under him in that Department, whether the Government was in possession of any correspondence between Mr. Wrightson and Mr. Chadwick?

The Colonial Secretary: I did not.

"Port of Spain Gazette."
November 8th, 1931.

Witness **the interminable delay in even acknowledging** the Catholic Archbishop's protest made in April, 1930.

"Port of Spain Gazette."
November 15th, 1931.

The final telegram of refusal is said to have been received from the Secretary of State on the 17th of October last, but its contents are communicated to Captain Cipriani only on the 6th November— fully twenty days after receipt of the telegram! The draft Bill was issued [on] November 2nd and published on the following day; so that, by that date, the negative result of the representations to the Secretary of State was a matter for inference. But, in the evident desire of the Government to impose its will upon the public, and that in the crudest and most galling manner, the act of ordinary, common decency, of even forwarding the reply to Captain Cipriani on at least the same date as that of the issue of the draft Bill, seems to have involved too stupendous an effort! But perhaps, **as in the case of the reply to His Grace the Archbishop, the papers had been mislaid!**

When the Government did decide to give some information there was in 1903, as in 1931, the same ungraciousness in holding it back until the last minute, so as to handicap those who were asking for it.

Proceedings of Riot Commission.

Mr. Alcazar: Mr. Wrightson could have proposed the draft Ordinance which is now under enquiry long before March, 1903. He had ample time to do so, yet . . . . it is left until the time when it is impossible . . . . to have it properly discussed, and it is only then that it is introduced.

From the Colonial Secretary in reply to a request
for publication of despatches.

Relevant extracts . . . . from the despatches . . . . will be embodied by the mover of the Bill **in his speech on the second reading.**

There was then, as in 1931, the same carelessness in actual official documents having important bearing on the controversial issue.

Proceeding of Riot Commission.

Mr. Warner: Have you any thing to say with regard to that?

The Colonial Secretary: Yes. You will remember that the cross-examining Counsel asked me a number of questions yesterday as to the four million gallons .... He referred me to Hansard .... But I have since ascertained that anything to say with regard to that **was misprint for three million gallons, and the Director of Public Works left the Colony on vacation a few days afterwards, and had no opportunity of correcting Hansard.**

In the Legislature.

December 11th, 1931.

Acting Colonial Secretary: May I explain, Sir. When I wrote to Captain Cipriani I used the word "predecessor," but on page 4 of the correspondence you will see "predecessors." Those telegrams come in code, and the same code word serves for both the singular and the plural. **On re-reading the correspondence, it was quite clear that** the word used in this case was meant to indicate the plural—"predecessors."

Captain Cipriani: .... **The addition of an "s" in this particular instance is a very serious addition. It alters the whole situation.....**

On each occasion there was the same tactless and unnecessary baiting of the people by using authority to deprive them of their legitimate rights.

Public Notice.

1903.

Public notice is hereby given that in consequence of the limited accommodation of the Council Chamber .... admission .... will in future be given by ticket only ....

Tickets will be granted to applicants to the extent of the available sitting accommodation and no further ....

Tickets must be given up to the door-keeper on entrance ....

[As might have been expected, the Government packed the hall with clerks, officials and friends. This as much as anything else helped to precipitate the riot.]

Reply to letter.

1931.

> M. Hamal-Smith, Esq.,
> Vice President,
> Catholic Social Union.

Dear Sir,

In reply to your letter of the first instant, respecting the running of special trains from Couva and Sangre Grande on the 11th idem, I have the honour to inform you that whilst the Government appreciates the fact that the majority of Catholics are opposed to the Divorce measure; it is considered that the bringing of large crowds into Port of Spain might be dangerous, inasmuch as they might prove difficult to control. I therefore regret that the application for the running of special trains cannot be conceded.

> I am, etc., etc.
> C. SADLER,
> General Manager of Railways

And finally, there was in 1903 as in 1931 the same ferocious official preparation for slaughter, not only public, which is understandable, but secret as well.

Proceedings of Riot Commission.

Mr. Alcazar: Do you know whether some members of the Council were armed on that day . . . . that any of them had revolvers amongst the officials?

The Colonial Secretary: I heard that one had. That is the only case I know of. He said something about it.

Captain Cipriani in the Legislature.

December 11th, 1931.

I know enough about Riot Acts not to make any foolish **demonstration or to lead unarmed people against two or three machine guns which lie in your office.**

[This in addition to the police under arms.]

There has been no upheaval in 1931 demanding a Commission. But had there been, it is not difficult to see that the Colonial Secretary and other officials would have been as unhappy under cross-examination in 1931 as they had been in 1903. On both occasions it would seem that they deliberately did everything in their power to exacerbate those who had dared to commit the terrible crime of opposing what the Government wished to introduce; or perhaps as is more likely, carried on in typical Crown Colony fashion, reponsible to nobody, sure of a majority in the Council, with armed police ready at hand, and cruisers within easy call by wireless.

Such are the parallels between 1903 and 1931. Yet on the whole the 1931 Government was far worse and far more incompetent in its handling of the situation than the 1903. To begin with, it had the warning of the 1903 agitation to go by. The Governor, shortly after his arrival in the island, had himself stated in a despatch dealing with the Divorce question that the political situation was not good. And since he had come, with all the excitement over the attitude of the Government in the Electric Company matter it had got worse. Then, too, the world situation had got worse. If the Governor and his advisers maintained any contact with the people they would have known that all those who read and talk about politics had taken much interest in the Cyprus question, and as usual, Crown Colony. Government had come in for some serious criticism, with inevitable comparisons between Trinidad and Cyprus. Mr. Gandhi's activities were filling every newspaper. A local paper published portraits. Another published a special article from him. Not only the Indians in Trinidad, but all coloured men follow Mr. Gandhi's activities with intense interest. The mistake that all these government officials always make is to believe that the people are not interested in these things. The people themselves, as people everywhere, do not say much, and that deceives the governing class. But certain ideas float about of which the people are vaguely conscious, the leaders acutely so. Then something happens which touches the people nearly, they are instantly in contact with the leaders, and what fools think is unexpected, but what in reality is inevitable takes place. The Government should have known all these things, and any sensible Government under these conditions and knowing the Divorce burden that it was carrying, would have at least been careful to keep relations smooth. Instead of that, the Government embarked on a series of adventures, designed apparently to create as difficult a milieu for the Divorce Bill as possible. First of all the Government decided to present £25,000 to the British Government. It is not that the more intelligent people are so bitter against giving anything to the British Government. They have given before, and will give again. We in Trinidad know that should this country find itself in serious difficulties to-morrow, the British Government, without being appealed to, would come to the rescue, as it has come in the past. The point is that at the time Trinidad could not afford it. The Government was pleading economy, cutting down salaries, objecting to necessary public works which would relieve the terrible unemployment, and yet at the same time giving away this amount of no service whatever to the British Government. Further, the method chosen, £5,000 a year for five years, was foolish in the extreme, because it robbed the gift of its only real support—that England was in a bad hole and needed money to get out of it. But granted the Government wanted to swagger and impress the Colonial Office, why, in the name of Heaven, choose this particular time? At the very next meeting of the Council, the Government made another blunder. Obviously stung by the dissatisfaction about the £25,000, it brought in a Bill to initiate a long-pending water-scheme to relieve a great deal of suffering in the island. In typically English fashion, it had waited until the last minute, and the Bill could not have come at a more unseasonable time; it looked all over as if it had been brought to the Council, not because the Government wanted to bring it, but as a sort of salve to the dissatisfaction aroused by the previous Meeting. But even that a Crown Colony Government could not handle without clumsiness. For the Bill was so insolently worded that some of the unofficial members, although as usual they congratulated the Government, asked that the wording should be changed. The original wording ran:—

> Resolved.—That this Council is of opinion that, notwithstanding the existing financial depression both world and local, the Central Water Supply Scheme should be proceeded with without delay; and recommends that if at any time owing to the cost of financing the scheme, it proves impossible to balance the annual budget, such additional taxation as may be necessary to attain that end should be imposed.

The Government had not even the common-sense or the self-control to disguise its feelings.

And then at the very next meeting, having carefully mined the ground over which it was to advance, the Government went over the top with the Divorce Bill. One stands aside and looks at these men who tell us that we are unfit to govern, and wonders at them. The whole situation could have been handled so differently.

If the officials could have brought in a Bill to start the Water Scheme one week after they had given the £25,000, what could have prevented them bringing it in one week, or, for that matter, one month before. In politics more than anything else you have to give and take, recede in order to advance. The people wanted the Water Scheme badly, first because half the Island wanted water, and secondly because it meant work. Even before it came to the Council, the Governor could have chosen some semi-official function and given a hint. Then the Colonial Secretary should have made one of his best speeches about the Government being actuated, not merely by a desire to give the people water, but also a wish to give the poor people employment in this time of distress. One thing is sure, that Captain Cipriani, the people's man, would have been extremely pleased, and would have said so in his emphatic way. Others would have spoken in the same strain. The Government had already promised to give as much of the work as possible to local men. At some seasonable moment in the debate the Governor could have stated that he had not forgotten the promise, and would see to that personally. There would have been much favourable comment and hope among the people. And a few weeks after the £25,000 gift might have come in (if it had to come in), and with careful handling slipped through far more easily and provoking far less comment than it actually did. But the Government, as all Crown Colony Governments, irresponsible and secure, simply charged through, kicking up its heels and with head down, butting away all obstacles. Never does a Crown Colony Government take the slightest trouble with the people. The people are dirt. It is concerned with the Colonial Office and nothing else. European governments will issue bulletins, more often than not full of lies. Nevertheless they are aware of the people. The people are the last thing a Crown Colony Government thinks about.

Never, from start to finish, did the Government make the slightest effort to manipulate the public. The great argument of the Catholics was that there was no demand. Each side was doing all sorts of fancy sums with the various sections of the population, and proving that it was in the majority. Yet the Catholics could claim with every justice that while there had been numerous petitions against Divorce, mass-meetings and various other protests and demonstrations, the pro-Divorce demand had not shown itself. The Government, if as it believed there was a demand, could easily have manipulated public expression of it. On the side of the advocates of Divorce were several able speakers and influential men. A hint or two from the Governor in the right quarter and one or two large meetings would have been organised at once, for in a Crown Colony one will always find influential men who will walk down Frederick Street in their drawers if the Governor should ask them to do so. The advocates of Divorce had the money and the brains to organise public meetings in various parts of the country, and they would have done it with alacrity to please His Majesty's Representative. Speeches would have been made, resolutions passed as to the necessity for Divorce in the country, with the usual loud applause and general excitement from people wishing to amuse themselves after a hard day's work. The Catholics would have been made to feel foolish, and would have lost half their confidence and much of their case. But, forgetting all the heat that a very recent House of Commons had got into over whether the Church should have a new prayer book or an old, forgetting the attitude of half the people of England as to whether their neighbours should go to the cinemas on Sunday or not, forgetting all these things, as they forget so many other things, the Englishmen in the Government merely looked upon the Catholics as benighted wretches agitating against sweetness and light, and who therefore needed a firm hand. Secure of their majority in the Council, of the policemen with guns, and of the cruisers within easy call by wireless, the Government was ready to do or die.

What saved the situation was that those who really cared about Divorce would not riot and those who would riot did not care about Divorce. Perhaps the greatest mistake that the 1931 Government made was to expect any rioting, and by making such ostentatious preparations to show everybody how fearfully frightened it was. The people were not frightened, for, despite all the notices in the papers and all the police under arms, as soon as the Council Chamber opened they rushed in and filled up the place. The Government was said to have been influenced by the undoubtedly violent speeches of Captain Cipriani. Captain Cipriani did certainly say many violent and many foolish things. They were not so violent perhaps as the things which were said on the Irish question in 1914 by Mr. Bonar Law (who became Prime Minister of England); by Sir Edward Carson (who became Attorney General); and by Mr. F. E. Smith (who became Lord Chancellor). The difference between those men and Captain Cipriani was that while they not only said what they did, but actually countenanced gun running and active preparations for revolution, Captain Cipriani, after telling the Governor in the Council that if he continued with what he was doing he would find himself in Queer Street, went out into Port of Spain and in discussing the projected demonstration kept on telling everyone: "Mind you, come and demonstrate and show your disapproval because it is your privilege to do so. But keep order, and if you hear that anything is happening anywhere don't even go to see, but find yourselves straight home." Captain Cipriani is a soldier, and no soldier encourages rioting of any sort. He leaves that for civilians who do not know what the actualities of these things are. Further, who was to do this rioting? The Catholics asked for special trains for their people to come into Port of Spain, people dressed in their best clothes—husbands, wives and children, accompanied by priests, a congregation of congregations. To spread the belief that such people in Trinidad would riot was a wicked slander. No man is going to start rioting when he has his family there with him. Had the demonstration been in connection with unemployment or a strike for increased wages, or anything of the kind in which the lowest classes of the population would have felt themselves nearly concerned, or would have listened to agitators bent on violence, then the Government could have had reason for the attitude if adopted. But the people in any community who would riot (if goaded to it by incompetent administrators and especially by martial preparations flaunted in their faces), such people were not interested in divorce. The Workingmen's Association gave Captain Cipriani a mandate against Divorce, but those were the leaders, the chosen representatives of the various subject associations. They gave Captain Cipriani a mandate because they didn't care very much about the matter one way or the other. He is their man for Self-Government and for Trade Unions, the man who stands for them and their point of view, and if he wanted a mandate against Divorce, well, they would give him one, especially when the method of the Government in going through with the Bill reminded them so much of its methods in regard to the things they are fighting for. Had the Government been in touch with the people it would have known what everybody else knew. But, as will be shown in a succeeding volume, from the very beginning of Crown Colony Legislature to the preesnt day, its methods have been always the same. At the very first sign of unrest of any kind, it behaves in a way calculated to increase the turmoil, being often directly responsible for it, and then when everything is finished sends or carries home reports about the excitable nature of the negro people.

———

Captain Cipriani took one view when the Divorce question first came up, and on second consideration he took another. There is nothing strange in that, nothing unique. It is a thing that happens over and over again, in the ordinary affairs of human life, in business, in politics, in fact wherever man has to use that uncertain and fallible weapon, his judgment. There is no need to insult the intelligence of readers with a list of persons who in recent political history have changed their minds, not like Captain Cipriani on a question of divorce (for Trinidad) which had come up rather suddenly, but on political views which they had held and expounded for many years. Naturally, his political opponents made very much use of what he had said on former occasions and what he said afterwards. It was natural and fitting that they should do so, and they would have been very foolish not to take the chance, but that Captain Cipriani should be looked upon as if he had been guilty of some act of treachery or moral aberration is a political but not a reasonable view.

For one thing in this Divorce matter he is to be censured. He allowed himself to say things against his opponents which should never have come from him above all persons, who having been formerly on their side should have been able more than anyone else to appreciate their point of view.

But we can leave Captain Cipriani alone for a moment. What should concern everyone interested in the constitution question, Catholic or non-Catholic, is not so much the fact of Divorce being introduced into the Colony, but the method by which it was done.

We approach the end, and it is fitting that we conclude with a clear view of the machinery of Crown Colony Government at work.

It has been stated that the officers responsible for the government of the Colony did not wish to bring in any Divorce Bill whatever, were well aware of the strength of the opposition which the introduction of such a Bill would arouse, and would have been glad to leave it alone. Let there be no doubt about this. Between 1926 and to-day three persons have acted as Governors of the Colony: Sir Horace Byatt, Mr. Grier and Sir Claud Hollis. Sir Horace Byatt wrote:

In this, as in certain other colonies, public opinion has hitherto been on the whole opposed to the introduction of a Divorce Law or at least has seen no necessity for it.

That was in 1926, and nothing that has happened between 1926 and to-day has shown that that opinion is to any extent invalid.

Mr. Grier, who acted as Governor after Sir Horace, whatever may be his views on divorce, was careful as Colonial Secretary to vote against the measure, showing at least that he respected the strength of the public opinion which was against it.

When Sir Claud Hollis came to Trinidad, and the question was put to him, this was the opinion he formed.

> I did not, however, consider that it would be politic immediately on my arrival in the colony to sponsor a measure which is certain to raise a storm of opposition by both the Roman Catholic and Protestant communions.
>
> And a little later in the same dispatch:
>
> I feel that it would be asking for trouble at a time like this, when the political atmosphere is none too peaceful, deliberately to raise this hornet's nest.

Here we have incontrovertible evidence of what the opinion of the Government has been from the very beginning of the Divorce question to the present time. To suggest that at any time after 1926 there has been any demand for divorce is merely playing with words. It is quite true that in a question of this kind one does not expect a demand in the sense that one would expect a demand for Trade Union Laws or for Representative Government. Mr. O'Reilly here made one of the few argumentative errors of his able speeches. He said that there was no demand for the emancipation of the slaves in 1834. But there was. There was the insistent demand of the British public itself. But the

British public is not interested in divorce for Trinidad. Mr. O'Reilly said also that there was no demand for emancipation in America. There was. For example, the anti-slavery newspaper, "The Liberator," founded in 1831, and the American Anti-Slavery Society, founded in 1833, a generation before the Civil War. There was practically nothing in Trinidad.

The trifling agitation during the last fortnight before the actual passing of the Bill was confined almost entirely to a few persons, whose writings on the subject need only the slightest examination to show that the motives which moved many of them were not so much pro-Divorce as anti-Catholic.

The Colonial Office, however, was insistent. Why it was so insistent is hard to say, except perhaps it was the capriciousness bred of unlimited power. Mr. Amery's dispatch will not bear examination for one minute. He wrote:

> General colonial and imperial practice and experience is relevant to this question which cannot properly be regarded as a purely local one. Local public opinion, whatever it may be, must of course carry considerable weight, but there is decided difficulty in gauging that opinion in such a matter as this in which social custom is held by them to be inseparable from religious belief, etc., etc.

There is not a word there which could not have been written by a Secretary of State in regard to Divorce for the people of Ireland before the formation of the Irish Free State. Yet to-day neither Ireland nor Quebec has divorce. What, then, about general colonial and imperial practice and experience? What, then, about social custom being inseparable from religious belief? The people of Ireland and the people of Quebec have far more right to the term "people of the British race" than the vast majority of the people of Trinidad and Tobago, who have no right to it at all. Would Mr. Amery, or for that matter any other minister, dare to speak to the people of Canada, of Australia or South Africa about "general colonial and imperial practice?" for he does not confine himself to colonial, but distinctly says general colonial and imperial. Surely those who are glad that the Divorce Bill has passed and those who are sorry can see the far more vital issue which is at stake.

But to continue with Mr. Amery:

A large number of people who have not given adequate consideration to the sociological aspect may easily be led to sign petitions which give an illusory impression.

And later:

The views of the members of Council who have taken a marked interest in the question seem to me to constitute probably the best guide to local opinion as being the views of leading men who are mainly concerned with the general social effects involved.

And yet plain for all the world to see is the fact that every Catholic among these leading men who "were mainly concerned with the general social effects involved," and who have taken "a marked interest in the question," every Catholic, including the Attorney-General, voted against the Bill. Sir Wilfred Jackson, the former Colonial Secretary, a Catholic, would most certainly have voted against the Bill. Mr. Amery would have us believe that the petitions were signed by persons who had not considered the matter, and the men on the Council voted against it because they had given adequate consideration to the sociological aspect. He is quite wrong. From the Attorney-General down to the humblest opponent in Sans Souci, though according to intelligence and education they would see more or see less of the question and all that it involved, yet were most strongly influenced by the fact that they were Catholics and had grown up with the belief that Divorce was against the principles of the Catholic Church.

From every aspect this question displays the inadequacy of the system of Crown Colony Government, as it is bound to be displayed at any crisis. The leaders of the Government tried to put a bold face on the matter and carry it through on their own, but despite their overwhelming majority in the Council, their hearts failed them at the last minute. The Solicitor-General in the final debate read out with great unction and more to the people in the Hall than to the members of the Council the instructions of the Secretary of State for the Colonies. He seemed entirely unaware of the moral feebleness of the position that he was adopting, for what he was saying to the people of Trinidad was in essence this: "Do not blame us. It is not our fault. We cannot help it. Listen for yourselves. We are under orders."

One despatch said that the official vote would not be used and all members could vote as they pleased. But in what way would a body of English

Protestants vote? And would any group of officials have flouted their superior by throwing out a Bill which he had been so insistent should be brought in? That was the force underlying the violence of the Catholic opposition. Powerful and numerous as it was, it was beaten before the battle began. And a country that is governed in that way is badly governed.

Finally there is the biggest question of all.

Let anyone get a copy of these despatches, or at least of the scraps of them that have been vouchsafed to the public, and read them through dispassionately. As he does so, a certain aspect of them cannot fail to strike him forcibly. This is the way they go.

> Sir Horace Byatt:
> . . . . . I considered so important a change. . . . .
> I need hardly say that I shall have no objection. . . . .
> Mr. Amery:
> I am of the opinion that the early introduction in Trinidad of a general law of divorce. . . . .
> Sir Horace Byatt:
> I do not consider that the time is yet ripe. . . . .
> Mr. Amery:
> I feel that an interval sufficient . . . . .
> And so right through from beginning to end.

Now, making all allowances for the advice His Excellency received from his Council, etc., and all that Mr. Amery read about the subject, it is painfully obvious that in the last resort this question of Divorce affecting a community of 400,000 people was settled by two men, both of them of a race different to the majority of the people whom the legislation affected, one of whom had never in his life seen the colony of Trinidad, and the other, who had had nothing whatever to do with it until he came here as Governor, and would have nothing whatever to do with it when his period as Governor was over, except a pensionable and perhaps a sentimental interest. The thousands of reasonably well educated and intelligent persons of some standing in this community, how do they feel when they read these despatches and recognise the assumptions on which they are based?

Yet maladministration brings its own reward. For the Divorce question has left the island shaken and the prestige of the Government has received a severe shock. The Government knows now what it should have known before, that such tension, the arming of police, the fierce denunciations of the rival speakers, the old sores exposed, the old grievances recalled, the threats and counter-threats, disturb the political atmosphere and leave behind unrest and bitterness in which spring up and flourish strange growths. Governments, especially alien governments, should never clash directly with any large and influential section except the clash is absolutely unavoidable. It is rumoured that after the Divorce agitation the Governor received a telegram from the Home Government, instructing him to avoid conflict with the people. If the telegram did not exist, then it was necessary to invent it. Should any agitation spring up in the near future, though unconnected with Divorce, the Government will find how much its handling of the Divorce question has tied its hands.

––––––

No one would vote more quickly for Divorce than the writer. But Divorce is a domestic matter and, to anyone with his eyes on the constitution question, Divorce is a trifle. People are apt to be short-sighted in these matters. Italy has no Divorce. That is Italy's business. England's Divorce laws lag hopelessly behind any intelligent conception of Divorce Legislation. That is England's business. France to this day cannot see its way to give its women the vote. That is France's business. Conservatism on social issues is not confined to the West Indies as some provincials think. Had Trinidad been reasonably governed the pro-Divorcists, if they felt so strongly on the matter, would have had to organise their forces to get public opinion on their side, and then get to work. Harm might have been done, but with Divorce as with any other matter, the people must work these problems out themselves. In no other way can they gain experience; and the wisdom and strength and confidence which come from experience.

No public man is more widely known in Trinidad to-day than Captain Cipriani, but as this book will be read by other than Trinidadians it is just as well to complete the picture.

He is below middle height, very solidly built and giving at first glance an impression of squareness and power. He has a big fleshy clean-shaven face, and his eyes, of a peculiar greenish colour, though small, sometimes in conversation, and always in public speech blaze with a fire which increases the impression of force so characteristic of his general appearance.

He wears always a khaki suit of military cut, brown boots, and a white helmet. There is no democratic affectation in this. That simplicity has always been his way. (But he does not wear the same in London. When the boat leaves Barbados he dons the regulation tweeds).

For his living he still trains horses and is also an auctioneer. During the day he can always be found in a dusty auctioneer's office in St. Vincent Street. But he does very little auctioneering and his chief business is his politics. He has a cocoa estate, but although himself a planter, his political work caused him to neglect it so much that had not two of his supporters taken it over he would have lost it long ago.

He represents the people so well, chiefly because he is so much one of them. All through the day persons pass in and out, coming to see him usually for help of some kind, some with grievances, some with information, some asking for advice, many begging. They stop him in the street. They pursue him to his house, for his purse is always open.

"Captain, will you please, . . . ?" "Captain, I am very sorry, but . . . ." "Captain, I don't want to trouble you, but . . . . ." And the shillings and sixpences change hands.

"Captain, will you look at this list?"

"Certainly." (A cursory glance). "Here is five dollars."

The man to whom he is talking smiles.

"But, tell me, did you read it? Do you know what it is for? I am sure you didn't see."

"No. But I know the fellows, and I am sure it is a good cause." And that was long before the Corporation decided to pay the Mayor for his services. Local industry, the local man doing anything to improve himself or improve the state of the country, that is his particular weakness. Two men come to him asking for his patronage in an effort to place before the public some pottery locally made.

Yes, the Captain will give them his patronage. Also he will help them by paying for the hall and for the lights. On the appointed night he is there as Mayor of the City, doing all he can to bring the work of these men before the public, though he is leaving for England in a few days, and has Workingmen's Association Elections on, and the Estimates of the Corporation, and a thousand things beside.

In ordinary conversation he speaks with a drawl, and rather surprisingly, except on political topics, is a very quiet man, sure of himself, but unaggressive in style. As an orator, however, he is the best in Trinidad, and one of the best we have had here for many years. Not as polished as some, not as scholarly as others, lacking the intellectual adroitness of legal training; yet he excels in the first duty of every public speaker: to convince his hearers that he means what he says, which, added to his sound common-sense and his knowledge of the life of the people, makes him so effective. You may see him addressing an audience of an old man of seventy and a jockey with all the energy and vigour that he addresses himself to the Legislature or a public meeting of his own Association.

He sits in the Legislative Chamber very quietly smiling at every attack that is made against him. Often he fans and frequently he wipes his head with a backward gesture which usually characterises bald-headed men, though he has all his hair. Rarely has he any notes, still less rarely does he make any, though he will hold a pen and draw lines about a paper in an aimless way. And the stronger the attack the more he smiles. But when his turn comes, his face almost at once becomes almost deadly serious. He gives a little cough, and then he begins. However dull the debate, however sleepy and bored the members may be, the moment Captain Cipriani stands on his feet the Council is alive.

There is yet another side to his efforts. Whenever he speaks on public matters, in private or in public, he shows and inspires an intense love of his own country. Hear him speaking to the children:

> This Trinidad of ours has got a future before her; from her geograph-ical position she is going to prove, I feel, one of the most important stations in this part of the civilised world, stationed as she is between North and South America. Her future is something which we cannot conceive at the present moment . . . . . and I beg you to make your-selves ready when that time comes . . . . . to do what we expect you to do, to put every effort in the development, economically, politically, and in every other way in the great future that lies before Trinidad and her people.

And on another occasion:

> To-day we have our Trinidad, to which we are all so proud to belong. The proudest boast of the Englishman is that his home is his castle, and if I can be satisfied that I can imbue the same spirit into the souls of our children, boys and girls, who will be the men and women of to-morrow, to make your West Indian homes your castles, or your Trinidadian homes your castles, then I feel that a great and good work will have been well and truly done.

He does not only work himself, but he gives them inspiration. He has made the people aware of politics as never before. But not only from the mean motive of self-interest. He tries and does succeed in making them feel the part that they ought to take in the development of their country. He tries to impress upon them, not only their privileges, but their duties as citizens. He tries to instil a proper pride in themselves, to make them feel their importance in the structure. And in this necessary part of the work of any modern community he stands almost alone. For from those who benefit most from the form of government and who enjoy all its privileges, the people get no inspiration of any kind, nothing except to jump to attention when the British National Anthem is played.

Despite many minor blemishes, his speeches sometimes achieve amazing rhetorical effect.

It is all very well and good to talk of us as "subject races." I laugh that to scorn. We are free people of the British Empire. We are entitled to the same privileges and the same form of Government and administration as our bigger sisters, the Dominions, and we have got to use everything in our power, strain every nerve, make every effort—I go further and say to make every sacrifice to bring self-government and Dominion status to these beautiful Colonies.

"Shoulder to shoulder," "strain every nerve," "irrespective of class, colour or creed," "fair play for the under-dog," phrases that died many years ago, but when he uses them as he so often does, they live again, vitalised not only by his magnificent voice, but by the fire of the convictions and the strength of the personality behind them.

It looks sometimes as if the struggle is hopeless, for often he does not get the support in quarters where he has reason to expect it. His enemies are powerful and on the alert to down him, and he too often gives them a chance by the violence and intemperance of his language. He will say that if he raises his finger he can cause a riot. Which is true, and therefore is all the more reason why he should not say it, especially as he would be the last man to attempt any such folly. Knowing the strength of the opposition, he should be more careful, for they miss no chance, and doubtless these statements of his are stored up for future (if not present) use. Because he has opposed Divorce, his enemies do their best to show that the man who has striven so unceasingly for the people, for representative government, for Trade Union Laws, for poor relief, for better housing, for more education, his enemies try to prove that now he is against the people. On this subject even a man like Mr. O'Reilly grows lyrical and quotes poetry, but though the people are sometimes foolish, they are not so foolish as all that, and their reply to all the prophecies of failing influence with the working man was to elect him unanimously as President for the coming year. To-day, as from the beginning, they are solidly with him.

He is in the thick of the fight and it is certain will continue to the end. If even he has to stand and see many things get past him, yet it is worth much that he is there on guard, ready to go to the last extremity against the atmosphere of Crown Colony Government which has stifled the people for so long. Some future Strachey of the West Indies will amuse his generation by fanciful speculation as to the real motives. We who know him can pass a simple judgment. He has felt the wrongs of the people like his own, seeking neither money nor influence nor place, but, gifted with splendid powers, has used them splendidly in perhaps the best of all causes, clearing a path for the self-realisation of his countrymen. Democracy, dictatorship, of a group or of the proletariat, it does not matter; a people like ours must be free to make their own failures and successes, and develop themselves in their own way. Otherwise, they remain without credit abroad and without self-respect at home, unable to achieve any unity or national consciousness, a bastard feckless conglomeration of individuals, inspired by no common purpose, moving to no common end.

The final phase of Captain Cipriani's work may fitly be brought in here. He has been often in England during the last few years, and if he is still at liberty and his activities not yet suppressed it is because of the friends he has made in London. At the Labour Commonwealth Conference in July, 1930, he made perhaps the finest speech of his career. It is impossible to quote it all here, and perhaps quotation has already been too lavish, but a contemporary biographer should never speak when his subject can speak for himself and this speech is Captain Cipriani's credo. The writer can well remember the thrill of pride which ran through the community when it was reported in the local newspapers.

> The first question is the important one of self-government for the West Indies, and our claim to this right is the reasonable and practical one that we have the education, ability, culture, and civilisation, necessary to undertake and successfully administer the affairs of our country. I here call attention to the promises made in "Labour and the Nation" that self-government would be immediately granted to those Colonies demanding it. We were reminded of those promises by Miss Lawrence yesterday in her inspiring address, and told by that lady that the Labour Government was endeavouring to fulfill them as quickly and fully as possible. Unfortunately, however, in our case, neither this nor any other promise has been fulfilled or lived up to, and we regret very much to have to remark that Labour in opposition gave us much more help and support than Labour in Power. . . .

It is quite true that the natives or inhabitants of the West Indies are, in the majority, coloured people, but they are coloured gentlemen, highly cultured and educated, having the same aims and aspirations as the white man: men, educated in your Public Schools, taking their professions in your Inns of Court, your Universities and Hospitals, and it is this class that is now forced to put up with the big stick autocracy of the official from Africa.

A great deal was made two days ago of the question of Trusteeship by Mr. J. H. Thomas in his opening address; too much altogether is being made of this. We cannot always be held in leading strings by the Colonial Office, and we want to be perfectly plain and say that we are fed up with Crown Colony rule, and are not prepared to carry on this one-sided and sordid partnership which proves of interest only to the one partner, and that is—the friends and relatives of the Colonial Office.

It will, no doubt, come as a great surprise to hear that this Government has, within the past six months, refused the introduction of Trade Union Laws in Trinidad. I ask myself whether I understand aright the situation as I take it that you, and consequently, we, are a Labour and Trade Union Government, and if that is so, how can one reconcile the action of your Trade Union Government in refusing Trade Union Laws to themselves and their comrades. If a Trade Union is something beneficial to the workers of England and of general application throughout the United Kingdom, how can they be hostile and opposed to good government and the best interests of the people of the West Indies and in Trinidad? The introduction of Trade Union Laws was held out to us as far back as the days of the Wood Commission, and the question has been asked from time to time while the Conservative Government was in power. Each time it was turned down, and I admit that under Tory rule one expected to have it turned down. But I am at a loss to understand how a Labour and Trade Union Government in power refuses to allow their introduction, and I would be grateful if any member of this Government, of the Labour Party or of the T.U.C., could throw any light on this anomaly. . . .

If Trinidad were allowed to make advantageous use of her mineral resources, as she could well do, there never would have been the slightest necessity to approach the Imperial Government to ask for relief to carry on her Sugar Industry: and this extraordinary spectacle presents itself to the view: that the Colonial Office, having deprived us, as effectively as they could, of our most valuable assets, now take up the unreasonable and unfair attitude of treating us as though we were mendicants depending on the bounty of the English people. We are neither mendicants nor paupers begging for charity. We request to be given what is our own—viz., the mineral wealth of our country—and in this demand I look to you, my friends of the Dominions, as much as to my friends of the British Labour Party, for help and support to remedy a somewhat tragic position caused by a reckless indifference which would be incredible were it not true.

I am making representations to-day for a fair, honest and reasonable claim, and while I appreciate the difficulties with which the present Government are confronted, I say that difficulties are made to be overcome. What is required is better understanding, more intimate and reasonable examination of the situation. In the past, and even to-day, the information dealing with the Colonies, their needs, their requirements, their aims and aspirations, is got from the ordinary official channel through the capitalist clique, the plantocracy and the employer class, dished up and served out by the Colonial Office here. The voice of the people, the voice of the working man is never heard at all, and therefore I look forward to a Labour Government in Office and in power, for a change in this unfair and un-British treatment meted out to us by an autocratic regime; and I am to remind my friends of the Labour Party that the same class, the same weight of numbers of the working men and women that returned them to office and placed them in power, holding and controlling the reins of the present Commonwealth of Nations to which we belong, is the same class and the same vote that have returned me in my country as their representative: and on their behalf I am here to claim what are their legitimate rights and privileges, and more than that, I am entitled to a satisfactory and sympathetic hearing. The wrongs which I have enumerated against our country have been too long perpetrated upon a long suffering and inarticulate people. We have reached the cross-roads, and we state the case fairly, honestly, truthfully, and firmly, looking to you for help and support which must be granted by minds that are true and just. I cannot believe that yet another bitter disappointment awaits the loyal people of the British West Indies.

There were men there from all parts of the British Empire. None who heard but would carry away with him, not only a memory of the speaker, but some understanding of the place and people for whom he spoke.

———

Here for the time being we must come to an end. The above has been a Pisgah sight. How far Crown Colony Government was useful, its ineradicable defects, the astonishing variety of governments tried in the West Indies during the last hundred years, the differences from island to island, the only road to solution, these and kindred subjects will be dealt with in a succeeding volume.

THE CASE FOR WEST-INDIAN
SELF GOVERNMENT

| | | | |

TO

CAPTAIN ARTHUR A. CIPRIANI, *of Trinidad*

T. A. MARRYSHOW, *of Grenada*

J. ELMORE EDWARDS, *of Grenada*

C. D. RAWLE, *of Dominica*

Leaders of the democratic movement in the West Indies

CONTENTS

A Colonial Office Commission is now taking evidence in Trinidad, the Windward and the Leeward Islands, with a view to the federation of all or some of them. But in these islands to-day political unrest is widespread and deep, and Sir Philip Cunliffe-Lister, the Secretary of State for the Colonies, has consented to the request of a deputation that the Commission be allowed to take evidence on the constitutional question. Yet the merits and demerits of constitutions cannot be fairly adjudged without a thorough understanding of the social constituencies they serve. First, then, to give some account of the people who live in the West Indies—in the West Indies, for though the scope of the present Commission is restricted, yet British Guiana (for administrative purposes always considered a part of the West Indies) and Jamaica are closely watching, and the decision of the Colonial Office will powerfully affect opinion and action in these colonies.

The bulk of the population of these West Indian Islands, over 80 per cent., consists of Negroes or persons of Negroid origin. They are the descendants of those African slaves who were brought almost continuously to the West Indies until the slave trade was stopped in 1807. Cut off from all contact with Africa for a century and a quarter, they present to-day the extraordinary spectacle of a people who, in language and social customs, religion, education and outlook, are essentially Western and, indeed, far more advanced in Western culture than many a European community.

The advocates of Colonial Office trusteeship would have you believe that the average Negro is a savage fellow, bearing beneath the veneer of civilisation and his black skin, viciousness and criminality which he is losing but slowly, and which only the virtual domination of the European is able to keep in check. Says Lord Olivier[1]:

"In the matter of natural good manners and civil disposition the Black People of Jamaica are very far, and, indeed, out of comparison, superior to the members of the corresponding class in England, America or North Germany."

Of their alleged savagery:

"This viciousness and criminality are, in fact, largely invented, imputed and exaggerated in order to support and justify the propaganda of race exclusiveness."

The trustees would have you believe that even when he is not a savage the average Negro is a simple, that is to say, a rather childish fellow. Compare this with Lord Olivier's opinion (among those of a hundred others), that:

"The African races generally have a subtle dialectical faculty, and are in some ways far quicker in apprehension than the average Caucasian. . . .

"The African, whether at home or *even in exile after the great hiatus of slavery*,[2] shows practical shrewdness and aptitude for the affairs of local government. His legal acumen is higher than that of the European."

The last argument of the trustees, even when they have to admit the attainments of the Negro, is that he does not produce sufficient men of the calibre necessary for administering his own affairs. Yet Sir Charles Bruce,[3] after his wide experience could say:

"In the meantime, such has been the energy and capacity of the Afro-European population in the Crown Colonies, where they form the bulk of the general community, that there is no department of Government, executive, administrative, or judicial, in which they have not held the highest office with distinction, no profession of which they are not honoured members, no branch of commerce or industry in which they have not succeeded."

---

[1] Lord Olivier: Secretary of the Royal W.I. Commission of 1899; Governor of Jamaica (1907–13); Chief Commissioner, W.I. Sugar Commission, 1930.
[2] Italics my own.
[3] Served in many Colonies, including the Windward Islands; at one time Governor of British Guiana.

To-day and at any time during the last forty years such posts as Chief Justice, Colonial Secretary, Puisne Judge, Attorney-General, Solicitor-General and Surgeon-General could be filled two or three times over by local men, most of them men of colour. The Civil Services are over 90 per cent. coloured, and even in large-scale business, the white man's jealous preserve, numerous coloured men occupy high and important positions.

It has to be admitted that the West Indian Negro is ungracious enough to be far from perfect. He lives in the tropics, and he has the particular vices of all who live there, not excluding people of European blood. In one respect, indeed, the Negro in the tropics has an overwhelming superiority to all other races—the magnificent vitality with which he overcomes the enervating influences of the climate. But otherwise the West Indian people are an easy-going people. Their life is not such as to breed in them the thrift, the care, and the almost equine docility to system and regulation which is characteristic of the industrialised European. If their comparative youth as a people saves them from the cramping effects of tradition, a useful handicap to be rid of in the swiftly-changing world of to-day, yet they lack that valuable basis of education which is not so much taught or studied as breathed in from birth in countries where people have for generation after generation lived settled and orderly lives. Quicker in intellect and spirit than the English, they pay for it by being less continent, less stable, less dependable. And this particular aspect of their character is intensified by certain social prejudices peculiar to the West Indies, and which have never been given their full value by those observers from abroad who have devoted themselves to the problems of West Indian society and politics.

The Negroid population of the West Indies is composed of a large percentage of actually black people, and about fifteen or twenty per cent. of people who are a varying combination of white and black. From the days of slavery, these have always claimed superiority to the ordinary black, and a substantial majority of them still do so (though resenting as bitterly as the black assumptions of white superiority). With emancipation in 1834 the blacks themselves established a middle class. But between the brown-skinned middle class and the black there is a continual rivalry, distrust and ill-feeling, which, skilfully played upon by the European people, poisons the life of the community. Where so many crosses and colours meet and mingle, the shades are naturally difficult to determine and the resulting confusion is immense. There are the nearly-white hanging on tooth and nail to the fringes of white society, and these, as is easy to understand, hate contact with the darker skin far more than some of the broader-minded whites. Then there are the browns, intermediates, who cannot by any stretch of imagination pass as white, but who will not go one inch towards mixing with people darker than themselves. And so on, and on, and on. Associations are formed of brown people who will not admit into their number those too much darker than themselves, and there have been heated arguments in committee as to whether such and such a person's skin was fair enough to allow him or her to be admitted, without lowering the tone of the institution. Clubs have been known to accept the daughter and mother, who were fair, but to refuse the father, who was black. A dark-skinned brother in a fair-skinned family is sometimes the subject of jeers and insults and open intimations that his presence is not required at the family social functions. Fair-skinned girls who marry dark men are often ostracised by their families and given up as lost. There have been cases of fair women who have been content to live with black men but would not marry them. Should the darker man, however, have money or position of some kind, he may aspire, and it is not too much to say that in a West Indian colony the surest sign of a man's having arrived is the fact that he keeps company with people lighter in complexion than himself. Remember, finally, that the people most affected by this are people of the middle class who, lacking the hard contact with realities of the masses and unable to attain to the freedoms of a leisured class, are more than all types of people given to trivial divisions and subdivisions of social rank and precedence.

Here lies, perhaps, the gravest drawback of the coloured population. They find it difficult to combine, for it is the class that should in the natural course of things supply the leaders that is so rent and torn by these colour distinctions.

For historic and economic reasons, the most important of the other native groups are the white creoles.[1] The white creole suffers from two

---

[1]Many of the West Indian Islands are cosmopolitan, and East Indians form about twelve per cent. of the total population, though concentrated in Trinidad. But

disadvantages, one of which he understands, and the other of which he probably does not. The first is climate. It seems that the European blood cannot by itself stand the climate for more than two or three generations. Here and there the third and fourth generation may use wealth, early acquired, to bolster mediocre abilities into some sort of importance, but the West Indies, as the generations succeed each other, take a deadly toll of all those families from temperate climates which make their home permanently there.

The second disability of the white creole is less tangible but equally important. He finds himself born in a country where the mere fact of his being white, or at least of skin fair enough to pass as white, makes him a person of consequence. Whatever he does, wherever he finds himself, he is certain of recognition. But with this power goes nothing beside personal responsibility. Englishmen govern the country. The result is an atmosphere which cramps effort. There is not that urgent necessity for exceptional performance which drives on the coloured man of ambition, and the white creole suffers accordingly. But this is not a disease which is easily seen by those who suffer from it, nor is the disease, even when diagnosed, one for which the patient is likely to take the remedy.

Into this community comes the Englishman to govern, fortified (sometimes) by university degrees; and of late years by a wide experience in dealing with primitive peoples in Africa.

His antecedents have not been helpful. Bourgeois at home, he has found himself after a few weeks at sea suddenly exalted into membership of a ruling class. Empire to him and most of his type, formerly but a word, becomes on his advent to the colonies a phrase charged with responsibilities, but bearing in its train the most delightful privileges, beneficial to his material well-being and flattering to his pride. Being an Englishman and accustomed to think well of himself, in this new position he soon develops a powerful conviction of his own importance in the scheme of things and it does not take him long to convince himself not only that he can do his work well—which to do him justice, he quite

---

there is no need to give them special treatment, for economically and educationally they are superior to the corresponding class in India; and get on admirably with the Negroes.

often does—but that for many generations to come none but he and his type can ever hope to do the work they are doing.

On his arrival in the West Indies he experiences a shock. Here is a thoroughly civilised community, wearing the same clothes that he does, speaking no other language but his own, with its best men as good as, and only too often, better than himself. What is the effect on the colonial Englishman when he recognises, as he has to recognise, the quality of those over whom he is placed in authority? Men have to justify themselves, and he falls heavily back on the "ability of the Anglo-Saxon to govern," "the trusteeship of the mother country until such time" (always in the distant future) "as these colonies can stand by themselves," etc., etc. He owes his place to a system, and the system thereby becomes sacred. Blackstone did not worship the corrupt pre-Reform constitution as the Colonial Office official worships the system of Crown Colony Government.

"Patriotism," says Johnson, "is the last refuge of a scoundrel." It is the first resort of the colonial Englishman. How he leaps to attention at the first bars of "God Save the King"! Empire Day, King's Birthday, days not so much neglected in England as ignored, give to his thirsty spirit an opportunity to sing the praises of the British Empire and of England, his own country, as its centre. Never does he seem to remember that the native place of the majority of those to whom he addresses his wearisome panegyrics is not England, but the colony in which they were born, in which they live, and in which they will in all probability die.

This excessive and vocal patriotism in the colonial Englishman is but the natural smoke of intensified fires burning within. That snobbishness which is so marked a characteristic of the Englishman at home, in the colonies develops into a morbid desire for the respect and homage of those over whom he rules. Uneasily conscious of the moral insecurity of his position, he is further handicapped by finding himself an aristocrat without having been trained as one. His nose for what he considers derogatory to his dignity becomes keener than a bloodhound's, which leads him into the most frightful solecisms.

In Grenada in 1931 there was a very orderly demonstration by all classes of the community against a decision of the Governor. One man who with his family had been invited to Government House for some social function took part in it. The Governor cancelled the invitation, but informed him that the cancellation did not apply to his wife and daughter who could come if they wanted to.

It is not surprising that the famous English tolerance leaves him almost entirely. At home he was distinguished for the liberality and freedom of his views. Hampden, Chatham, Dunning and Fox, Magna Carta and Bill of Rights, these are the persons and things (however misconceived) which Englishmen, undemonstrative as they are, write and speak of with a subdued but conscious pride. It is no accident, the Whig tradition in English historical writing. But in the colonies any man who speaks for his country, any man who dares to question the authority of those who rule over him, any man who tries to do for his own people what Englishmen are so proud that other Englishmen have done for theirs, immediately becomes in the eyes of the colonial Englishman a dangerous person, a wild revolutionary, a man with no respect for law and order, a self-seeker actuated by the lowest motives, a reptile to be crushed at the first opportunity. What at home is the greatest virtue becomes in the colonies the greatest crime.

The colonial Englishman it is fair to say retains some of the admirable characteristics which distinguish his race at home, but he is in a false position. Each succeeding year sees local men pressing him on every side, men whom he knows are under no illusions as to why he holds the places he does. Pressure reduces him to dodging and shifting. Thus it is that even of that honesty which is so well-recognised a characteristic of the English people,—but I shall let an Englishman speak: "It is difficult," says Mr. Somervell, the historian, "for white races to preserve their moral standards in their dealings with races they regard as inferior." Should Englishmen of fine sensibility stray into the Colonial Service they find themselves drawn inevitably into the circle of their colleagues and soon discover that for them to do otherwise than the Romans would be equivalent to joining a body of outsiders against their own. Thus it is that in the colonies, to quote an English official in the West Indies, "such large and intelligent classes of Englishmen come to have opinions so different from those for which the nation has ever been renowned at home."

In a Crown Colony Government all final decisions whatsoever rest with the Governor. To advise him he has an Executive Council consisting usually of his most important officials and one or two of the local population selected by himself. (But he can, if he wishes, act against even the unanimous advice of this Council.) Let us see a Governor and Executive Council at work to-day.

Just over thirty years ago the Government of Trinidad granted to a Canadian Company (registered locally as the Trinidad Electric Company) an exclusive monopoly for thirty years to generate and sell electric light and power and to conduct a tramway service within the city of Port-of-Spain. Neither to the Government nor to the Corporation did the Company pay anything for this privilege. In 1928, however, the City Council of Port-of-Spain began to discuss the position with the undisguised intention of ultimately acquiring the undertaking should the idea prove feasible. When approached by the City Council, Sir Horace Byatt, Governor, and Mr. Wilfred Jackson, Colonial Secretary, were sympathetic and decided on independent expert investigation. In March 1929 the Government recommended the services of Mr. Evan Parry as expert. Mr. Evan Parry, the Government stated, was a partner of the firm of Messrs. Preece, Cardew and Rider, and was due in Trinidad in November to give the Government advice on wireless questions. Inasmuch, however, as circumstances had caused the Government to require a wireless inspector at a much earlier date, the Government no longer needed Mr. Parry's services and the City Council could have him if it paid his expenses. The City Council agreed to have Mr. Parry.

Mr. Parry arrived at the end of November, 1929, but meanwhile Sir Horace Byatt and Mr. Wilfred Jackson had gone their ways, Sir Claud

Hollis and Mr. S. M. Grier taking their places. The Government appointed a committee consisting of the Attorney-General in the chair, the Government Director of Public Works, the Government Wireless Engineer, Captain Cipriani (the Mayor of Port-of-Spain and a member of the Legislative Council) and the Hon. Gaston Johnston, K.C. (five times Mayor of the City and also a member of the Legislative Council). A few weeks later the Government suggested that as the Company showed great unwillingness to give information the services of Mr. Harding should be secured, Mr. Harding having been until quite recently and for over twenty years manager of the Electric Company. The City Council agreed. The Government suggested that the City Council should pay Mr. Harding a retaining fee of a thousand dollars. To this also the City Council agreed.

The committee and Mr. Parry both reported that to take over the undertaking would prove profitable and that the Municipality should do so in preference to the Government.

About this time the President of the Trinidad Electric Company accompanied by Counsel came to Trinidad and soon after his arrival the Company made proposals to the Government limiting its earnings and providing for taxation. The Governor invited the Council to discuss the position.

Captain Cipriani, the Mayor, has since stated in public correspondence with the Government that before the Company communicated these proposals to the Government, Mr. S. M. Grier, the Colonial Secretary, had met the representatives of the Company at the Queen's Park Hotel, had assured them that if the Company made concessions he would win over the reasonable members of the City Council, and that the Government would sympathetically consider the extension of the franchise. Knowing what he knew, therefore, Captain Cipriani told the Governor that the City Council would not be a party to any three-cornered meeting. He said that the City Council wished to take over and the Government had encouraged it. To accept terms now would only mean the same situation arising before long. A few days after, the Colonial Secretary informed the City Council that the Government would not guarantee a loan for the purpose of the Council's acquiring, until a full investigation had shown that such acquisition would be in the public interest.

This talk of full investigation coming after the reports of the government committee and Mr. Parry stiffened the City Council and the Mayor issued a manifesto to the citizens. However, another deputation from the Council met the Governor again on June 17th. The Governor gave some figures (most of them supplied by the Company) in which he proved that it would be unprofitable for the City Council to take over. These figures included half a million dollars under the heading "cost of acquisition." The City Council decided to put the case before the Secretary of State for the Colonies; and a delegation was sent to England, the Company meanwhile taking the matter to the Courts. The delegation was met by Mr. Drummond Shiels, Under-Secretary of State for the Colonies, accompanied by Mr. Darnley, an official of the Colonial Office. During the discussion the delegation had to reply to three points. One was that there was a large excess of expenditure over revenue in the 1930 estimates of Port-of-Spain (which estimates had been approved by the Governor-in-Executive-Council without criticism or comment); another, that it was improper to get evidence from Mr. Harding (who had been recommended to the City Council by the Government); and thirdly, that the Government placed little value on the report of Mr. Parry (who also had been recommended to the City Council by the Government).

The implication that the financial position of the City Council was unsound irritated the delegation extremely, and it undertook to prove the reverse to Mr. Darnley, which it easily did. When the delegation again met Mr. Drummond Shiels, however, it was mystified to hear that he had since been informed that the City Council's financial position was sound. After the return of the delegation the City Council received a letter from the Colonial Secretary stating that in the event of the Company losing its appeal to the Privy Council the Government would offer no obstacle to the City Council's acquiring. The Company had claimed that by the ordinance it was entitled to its privileges in perpetuity. On January 4th, 1931, every claim of the Company was dismissed with costs. The Company appealed to the Privy Council.

The Government passed an ordinance, extending the franchise of the Company indefinitely, the Company meanwhile to enjoy all the profits. In conference, a City Councillor suggested protective legislation. Government delegates howled him down. In the Legislative Council debate

The deliberations of an Executive Council are secret. The body in which public interest centres is the advisory Legislative Council, which undoubtedly wields great influence, if not power. The Legislative Council of Trinidad is typical and will best serve as an example. This Council consists of three sections. The first is that of the official members, twelve in number, chosen by the Governor from among the various heads of departments. The second consists of the unofficial members, thirteen in number, partly nominated and partly elected. The third section is not the least important of the three—the Governor, who is in the Chair. It will be seen how potent for misgovernment is each of these three sections.

The official section, composed mainly of heads of departments, comprises a solid block of Englishmen with a few white creoles, generally from some other colony. These officials are for the most part strangers to the community which they govern; in Trinidad there have been five Attorney-Generals during the last dozen years. Their position is secure, and their promotion depends not on the people over whom they rule, but on a Colonial Office thousands of miles away. It is not difficult to imagine their bureaucratic attitude. There have been official members of the Trinidad Legislature who over a period of years have sat in the Council, saying nothing, doing nothing, wasting their own time and the time of the public. There is a further unreality, because whenever the Governor wishes he can instruct the officials all to vote in the same way. And the Council becomes farcical when two members of a committee appointed by the Governor receive instructions to vote against their own recommendations. Here to-day and gone to-morrow, these heads of departments, in clubs and social gatherings mix chiefly with the wealthy white creoles, whose interests lie with the maintenance of all the authority and privileges of the officials against the political advancement of the coloured people. Their sons and daughters intermarry with the white creoles and get employment in the big business houses. From all this springs that alliance so clearly foreshadowed by Cornewall Lewis. "We represent large interests," said the Attorney-General in a recent debate, and every West Indian knows the interests which he and the other officials represent. The local Government is the Chamber of Commerce, and the Chamber of Commerce is the local Government.

The unofficial members "representing the people" form the second group, and since 1925 they have consisted of six members nominated by the Governor and seven members elected by the people. Formerly the Governor nearly always appointed white men representing business interests. He might as well have appointed a few more heads of departments for all the representation the people got from them.

But it has been the policy of the Government for some years past to appoint a few Negroes to these positions. These have usually been Negroes of fair, and not of dark skin. And that type of man, whether on the Council or in the other departments of government, is often a more dangerous opponent of the masses of the people than the Europeans themselves.

In its broader aspect this is no new thing in politics. There is, first of all, the natural gravitation of all men towards the sources of power and authority, and, on far larger stages, parties of privilege have not yet ceased to hire mercenaries to do what would be less plausibly and effectively done by themselves. The West Indian Islands are small and the two easiest avenues of success are the help of the Government or the help of the white people. It is, therefore, fatally easy for the nominee to rationalise his self-seeking by the reflection that after all, in such a Legislature, he can achieve nothing that the Government sets its mind against.

There is yet another consideration no less powerful than the foregoing. These West Indian colonies offer especially to those no longer young, little in the way of organised amusement, and individuals are thrown back almost entirely on society for recreation. Mr. Julian Huxley, after four months' extensive travel in Africa, has written:

"Of a large and important section of white people in Africa, officials as well as settlers, it is not unfair to say that *The Tatler, Punch*, a few magazines, detective stories and second-rate romantic novels represent their intellectual and cultural level."

The case in Trinidad is precisely the same, and indeed the shallowness, the self-sufficiency and the provincialism of English colonial society has long been a by-word among cultivated persons. But it keeps itself to itself and thereby becomes exclusive. It is the wealthiest class, lives in the best houses, has the best clubs, organises the best amusements. For the fair-skinned Negro who does not seek much, that society seems a paradise.

But when that is said, though much is said, all is not said. There is first of all the Governor. There have been recent Governors whom the people despised, and rightly. Of one and his entourage it could be said that he represented the butler, his wife the housekeeper, and his A.D.C. the groom. But His Majesty's Representative is sometimes a man of parts, his wife a person of elegance. And whatever qualities they may have are naturally enhanced by the

"... power
Pre-eminence, and all the large effects
That troop with majesty."

Now and then among the officials one finds a really brilliant man. Of late, members of the Consular Body, and some of the Professors of the Imperial College of Tropical Agriculture, have contributed their fair share to local society. Distinguished visitors often lend both tone and colour to the social dullness of local life. Any unusual social talent of local origin, if it is white, will usually find its way to the top. Thus around the Governor centre a few small groups which, though they will vary in value from time to time, yet whatever they are, are by far the best that the islands can show, for the coloured people, though possessing in themselves the elements of a society of some cultural value (their range of choice being so much wider), are so divided among themselves on questions of colour, based on varying shades of lightness or darkness, that they have been unable to form any truly representative social group or groups. The result is that many a man conscious of powers above the average, and feeling himself entitled to move in the best society the island affords, spends most of his leisure time and a small fortune in trying to get as near to the magic centre as possible, in itself a not too mean nor too contemptible ambition. The serious flaw in the position of the local man of colour is this, that those to whose society and good graces he aspires are not only Englishmen, but Englishmen in the colonies, and therefore constitutionally incapable of admitting into their society on equal terms persons of colour, however gifted or however highly placed (unless very rich). The aspirant usually achieves only a part of his aim. The utmost sacrifice of money, influence, and dignity usually gains him but a precarious position on the outer fringes of the society which he hopes to penetrate, and he is reduced to consorting with those fairer than himself, whose cupidity is greater than their pride. Others who feel themselves above this place-at-any-price policy stand on their dignity and remain at home, splendidly isolated. Thus it is nothing surprising to find on the Legislative Council three or four coloured men, each a little different in colour, who are more widely separated from one another than any of them is from a white man, and whose sole bond of unity is their mutual jealousy in their efforts to stand well with the governing officials.

These matters would not concern us here except for their unfortunate reaction on the political life of the community.

Not only nominations to the Council but all appointments in the service are made by the Government, and the Government can, and usually does, point to the number of coloured men it has appointed. But either by accident or design it rarely appoints black men. The appointment of these fair-skinned men seems to depend to a large extent on the way, whether openly or covertly, they dissociate themselves from their own people. But those same arts a place did gain must it maintain. The result is that a more or less intelligent and aspiring minority occupy a position in which they do more harm than good, for to the Colonial Office and the ordinary observer, being men of colour, they represent the coloured people, while the Government and the white creole know that when it comes to a crisis these, their henchmen, are more royalist than the King. Some people have endeavoured to see in this a characteristic weakness of the coloured people and a grave reflection on their capacity for leadership. It is not so. Disinterested service actuated by nothing more than a sense of responsibility to one's own best convictions is a thing rare among all nations, and by necessity of less frequent occurrence in a small community of limited opportunities. These men are not so much inherently weak as products of the social system in which they live. Still, whatever the cause of their conduct, its effect is disastrous. Particularly as the Government will appoint a dark Negro to a position of importance only when it cannot get a fair one. In this way it builds up in the service a group of men who, however distasteful to Englishmen themselves, are at one with them in their common antipathy to the black. Despising black men, these intermediates, in the Legislative Council and out of it, are forever climbing up the climbing wave, governed by one dominating motive—acceptance by white society. It would be unseemly to lower the tone of this book by detailing with whom, when and how Colonial Secretaries and Attorney-Generals distribute the nod distant, the bow cordial, the shakehand friendly, or the cut direct as may seem fitting to their exalted Highnesses; the transports of joy into which men, rich, powerful, and able, are thrown by a few words from the Colonial Secretary's wife or a smile from the Chief Justice's daughter. But political independence and social aspiration cannot run between the same shafts; sycophancy soon learns to call itself moderation; and invitations to dinner or visions of a knighthood form the strongest barriers to the wishes of the people.

All this is, and has been, common knowledge in the West Indies for many years. The situation shows little signs of changing. The type of constitution encourages rather than suppresses the tendency. But the day that all fair-skinned Negroes realise (as some do to-day) that they can only command respect when they respect themselves, that day the domination of the coloured people by white men is over. If the white men are wealthy, they will have the influence of wealthy men. If they are able they will have the influence of able men. But they will cease to have the influence of wealth or ability, not because they are wealthy or able, but simply because they are white.

If we neglect the elected members for the time being (a form of attention to which they are well accustomed) there remains now only the Governor in the Chair.

At first sight it may seem that the Governor in the Chair occupies a merely formal position, but on closer observation it becomes immediately obvious that his position there is as mischievous as those of the other two sections of a Crown Colony Legislature. The Governor of a Crown Colony is three things. He is the representative of His Majesty the King, and as such must have all the homage and respect customary to that position. But the Governor is also the officer responsible for the proper administration of the government. The Governor-General of South Africa, like the other Governors-General, is not responsible for the government of the country. The responsible persons are the Prime Ministers of those countries. In Trinidad the Governor is Governor-General and Prime Minister in one. But that makes only two. When the Governor sits in the Legislative Council he is Chairman of that body. The unfortunate result is that when a member of the Council rises to speak he is addressing at one and the same time an incomprehensible personage, three in one and one in three. A Member of the House of Commons can pay all due respect to His Majesty the King, submit himself to the proper authority of the Speaker of the House, and yet express himself in uncompromising terms about any aspect of government policy which appears to him to deserve such censure. In a Crown Colony Legislature that is impossible. The Governor, being responsible for the administration, is liable to criticism directed against his subordinates. It is natural that he should, it is inconceivable that he would do otherwise than, defend those who assist him in carrying on the affairs of the Colony. But should a Governor make an inconvenient admission as the head of the Government he immediately assumes one of his other alibis. And in the Council as it is constituted and with the Governor holding the power that he holds, there are never lacking members always on the alert to jump to the defence of the dignity of His Majesty's representative or the respect due to the President of the Chamber, quite neglectful of the responsibility of the head of the administration. In December 1931 one nominated member in the course of his address on a Divorce Bill referred to the part the Governor had played in bringing forward that piece of legislation so unpopular with a certain section.

"It is a pity that Your Excellency did not publish these despatches earlier, so that the public might have known the part Your Excellency has played in respect to this matter. I have no doubt that now the despatches have been published and the atmosphere has been clarified, it will be realised that Your Excellency's share of the responsibility for the presentation of this Bill is absolutely nil.

"If I may say so without offence, it would appear that you are regarded by the Colonial Office merely as a servant of the centurion. . . . It must be very humiliating indeed to any responsible officer to find himself in the position in which Your Excellency must find yourself. . . . ."

Now that speech erred, if it erred in any way, on the side of temperance. The speaker was forcible, but, nominated brown-skinned Negro in a Crown Colony Legislature, his tone was so respectful as to be almost humble.[1] But not so in the eyes of one member. No. For him the Governor had been insulted. Nor did he wait for a government official to say so. He (himself a brown-skinned Negro) began his own address with a flood of compliment to the Solicitor-General (a white man) for the able way in which he had argued for the Bill and then turned his hose on the Attorney-General (another white man) and complimented him on the able way he had argued against the Bill. Then he switched off to the address of his brother Negro and nominated member.

"He referred to the Governor of this Colony in a way ill befitting any member of this Council. . . ."

Nor was he yet satisfied that enough sacrifices had been offered on the altar of the Governor's dignity. Before his speech was finished he found opportunity to make another salaam.

"I was pained to listen to his statement in almost flippant language that the Governor of this Colony was the servant of the centurion. . . ."

Instances may be multiplied. In his triple position the Governor in the chair exercises a disproportionate influence. His presence is a constant check to free expression of opinion. And a Legislative Council in which a man cannot freely speak his mind is a place fit for academic debates and not for the discussion of the affairs of government.

It is not difficult to imagine the result of all this in the working of the constitution. The Government, already so overwhelmingly strong, is without effective criticism or check, and being composed of men who are governing not for the sake of governing, but because they have to make a living, it is not strange that it should be as slack and regardless as it usually is. "Public life is a situation of power and energy. He trespasses upon his duty who sleeps upon his watch, and may as well go over to the enemy." There, Burke, as ever, master of political statement, distils for the politician a first principle.

---

[1] Alas! It did not save him. He has been omitted from the new nominations.

It is the lack of this active vigilance which robs our politics of any reality. Far from being alert guardians of the public weal, the favourite formula of most of these members is: "I beg to congratulate the Government." Should an official make a speech of no more than mediocre ability, each one, at some time in his own speech, "begs to congratulate the honourable member." Always they seem to be bowing obsequiously, hat in hand, always the oily flattery, the ingratiating smile, and criticism offered on a silver salver. A person gaining his first impression of politics from a reading of some of these debates would conclude not that it was the sole business of the Government to govern properly, but a favour that was being conferred upon the people. It must not be imagined that some of these members have been ciphers of no value on the Legislature. Sometimes they possess great ability or force of personality. They are men of the world enough to know that if to assert themselves too much is a mistake, it would be equally a mistake to assert themselves too little. But they can never have that full weight in public matters which comes from a man like Captain Cipriani, who speaks from his well-known and settled convictions, or from a respected Colonial Secretary who is stating the case from the Government point of view. Sometimes they find themselves inadvertently on the wrong side, and it is interesting to see them wriggle out. "Can the Government see its way to . . . ?" "No." "Couldn't the Government . . . ?" "No. . . ." "I still think I am right, however, though I beg to congratulate the honourable member who explained the Government's position. It is clear that the Government is quite right, too. I beg to congratulate the Government. The Government will hear nothing more of this from me."

One concrete example must be given of the attitude of these nominated representatives of the people.

From the time that the Imperial College of Tropical Agriculture started its work in Trinidad there were well-founded complaints of discrimination against coloured men. When, in April 1930, there came up before the Legislative Council a grant to the Imperial College of £8,500 a year for five years, Captain Cipriani asked the Government for a definite assurance that there would be no discrimination. If not, he would oppose the vote. Here for once the underlying reef was showing above the surface, plain, stark, and not to be denied.

The debate continued.

Mr. O'Reilly (who had had a brother there): "... I do not follow my honourable friend in suggesting that there has been any discrimination at the College...."

Sir Henry Alcazar: "... I do not propose to address you on the question of discrimination...."

The Colonial Secretary (reading a statement from the Principal of the Imperial College of Tropical Agriculture): "I am at a loss to know how the idea has occurred that there is a differentiation over coloured students...."

Dr. McShine: "Your Excellency, I also supported the desire to have some assurance from the College that the discrimination did not exist or that it was exaggerated, and I am glad to have the explanation, the statement of fact that it is not so...."

Mr. Kelshall: "I think that we ought in looking at this subject, to take a long view.... But I have the utmost confidence in the Head of the College —Mr. Evans —a broad-minded Englishman of the right sort... and I do not believe there is at present any ground for complaint in regard to discrimination among the students...."

Mr. Wortley (the Director of Agriculture): "I do feel strongly that the reason is not that the College does not wish them, but that for one reason or another the Trinidadians do not wish to go to the College. In other words, other professions and other openings attract them more...."

It remained for the Governor to conclude in the same strain:

"... We cannot dictate to private companies what appointments they should make, but it appears to me to be very foolish if Companies operating in the country do not appoint people that live there, and prefer to go elsewhere to fill appointments. If I can help in this matter I shall certainly do so." (Applause.)

So far the public debate. But what were the actual facts? Mr. Gaston Johnston (a coloured man), who was present, did not say anything in the House, but when the meeting was over he told Captain Cipriani that Father English, the Principal of St. Mary's College, had received a letter from Mr. Martin Leake, the previous Principal of the Agricultural College, in which Mr. Leake had asked Father English to discourage young men of colour from coming to the Imperial College, because although he, the Principal, had nothing against them, the white students made it unpleasant, which caused a great deal of difficulty.

"My God, Johnston, you mean to say you knew that and not only did not say so yourself, but did not tell me?"

"No, for if I had told you, you would say it and cause a lot of trouble."

Captain Cipriani knew, as every other member of Council knew, the true state of affairs at the College. When he went to England in the July following, he brought the matter to the notice of the Colonial Office. The Colonial Office official listened to him and then took up a copy of *Hansard*.

"Captain Cipriani, you complain of discrimination. Now, isn't Mr. O'Reilly a coloured man? Yes. Now listen to what he says.... Isn't Sir Henry Alcazar a coloured man? Now listen to what he says.... Isn't Mr. Kelshall a coloured man? ... Isn't Dr. McShine a coloured man? And this is what he says.... Now, Captain Cipriani, what have you come here making trouble about?"

Now one can understand the position of the white men who spoke in this debate. One can understand Mr. Wortley feeling so strongly that Trinidadians did not go to the Imperial College because they preferred other avenues, for it is an important part of the business of the Government official to deprecate any suggestion of colour discrimination, and, whenever the opportunity arises, to throw as much dust as possible. The same motives obviously actuated the Governor. How else is it possible to account for his apparent ignorance of the fact that the Oil Companies would as soon appoint a Zulu chief to some of their higher offices as a local man of colour, whatever the qualifications he had gained at the Imperial College? We can even pass over the irreconcilable conflict of evidence between Mr. Evans and his immediate predecessor. Englishmen or white men stand to gain nothing by talk about race discrimination; and on a short-sighted view they stand to lose a great deal. But in this debate, as in every other, what is so pitiful is the attitude of these so-called representatives of the people, who so often hold the positions that they do hold because of their colour. The majority of them hate even more than white men any talk about colour. For if they stand up against colour discrimination they will be noted by the Government as leaders of the people, and then good-bye to some of their dearest hopes; while for some it will mean facing in public the perfectly obvious but nevertheless dreadful fact that they are not white men.

That is the Trinidad Legislature. There is no room nor should there be need to go any farther into details of the course of legislation.

The reader may want to know more of that pitiful remnant, the elected members, who form usually about a third of the various Legislatures. The usual colour prejudices often divide them; and in any case it takes a man of the courage and strength of Captain Cipriani to hurl himself continuously against the solid phalanx arrayed against him. But the real hopelessness of the situation is best to be seen in Grenada and Dominica. In each of these smaller Islands, where the population is more homogeneous and more closely-knit, the local Government has achieved the astonishing feat of uniting both nominated and elected members against itself. In Grenada, both these groups, defeated by the official majority, retired from the Council. Warmly supported by the whole population they have returned, but certainly not to shed tears of happy reunion on the shoulders of the Government. In Dominica all the unofficials, nominated and elected, have refused to go back and though writs have been issued for a new election no one will stand. When, after a time, one man accepted nomination by the Government the people burnt his house down. It is in this way that Empires prod their citizens into violence and sow the seeds of their own dissolution. Yet though the writing on the wall stretch from Burma to Cyprus, there are those who will not read.

When will British administrators learn the lesson and for the sake of future cordial relations give willingly and cheerfully what they know they will have to give at last? How do they serve their posterity by leaving them a heritage of bitterness and hate in every quarter of the globe? Solution of the problem there is but one—a constitution on democratic lines. This does not necessarily mean a form of government modelled plastically on the English or Dominion systems. Ceylon shows one way, Malta another. The West Indian legislators have their constitution ready. That is not a matter for debate here. But there will only be peace when in each colony the final decisions on policy and action rest with the elected representatives of the people. Hard things are being said today about parliamentary democracy, but the West Indian Colonies will not presume to reject it until England and the Dominions show them the way. The high qualification for membership of the Council must go.

The high franchise for the power to vote must go. That tight-rope dancer, the nominated member, must vanish forever, and the representatives of the people thrown back upon the people.

No one expects that these Islands will, on assuming responsibility for themselves, immediately shed racial prejudice and economic depression. No one expects that by a change of constitutions the constitution of politicians will be changed. But though they will, when the occasions arise, disappoint the people, and deceive the people and even, in so-called crises, betray the people, yet there is one thing they will never be able to do—and that is, neglect the people. As long as society is constituted as it is at present that is the best that modern wage-slaves can ever hope to achieve.

For a community such as ours, where, although there is race prejudice, there is no race antagonism, where the people have reached their present level in wealth, education, and general culture, the Crown Colony system of government has no place. It was useful in its day, but that day is now over. It is a fraud, because it is based on assumptions of superiority which have no foundation in fact. Admirable as are their gifts in this direction, yet administrative capacity is not the monopoly of the English; and even if it were, charity begins at home, especially in these difficult times. The system is wicked, because to an extent far more than is immediately obvious it permits a privileged few to work their will on hundreds of thousands of defenceless people. But most of all is the system criminal because it uses England's overflow as a cork to choke down the natural expansion of the people. Always the West Indian of any ambition or sensibility has to see positions of honour and power in his own country filled by itinerant demi-gods who sit at their desks, ears cocked for the happy news of a retirement in Nigeria or a death in Hong-Kong; when they go and others of the same kind take their places, while men often better than they stand outside rejected and despised. And even were the Colonial Office officials ideally suited to their posts the situation would not be better, but worse than it is. For the more efficient they are, the more do they act as a blight upon those vigorous and able men whose home is their island, and who, in the natural course of events, would rise to power and influence. Governors and governed stand on either side of a gulf which no tinkering will bridge, and political energy is diverted into other channels or simply runs to waste. Britain will hold us down as long as she wishes. Her cruisers and aeroplanes ensure it. But a people like ours should be free to make its own failures and successes, free to gain that political wisdom and political experience which come only from the practice of political affairs. Otherwise, led as we are by a string, we remain without credit abroad and without self-respect at home, a bastard, feckless conglomeration of individuals, inspired by no common purpose, moving to no common end.

"Self-government when fit for it."

That has always been the promise. Britain can well afford to keep it in this case, where evidence in favour is so overwhelming and she loses so little by keeping her word.